VOICES IN LITERATURE

Mary Lou McCloskey • Lydia Stack

Heinle & Heinle Publishers • An International Thomson Publishing Company • Boston, Massachusetts 02116 U.S.A.

The publication of *Voices in Literature Bronze* was directed by the members of the Heinle & Heinle Secondary ESL Publishing Team:

Editorial Director: Roseanne Mendoza
Senior Production Services Coordinator: Lisa McLaughlin
Market Development Director: Ingrid A. Greenberg

Also participating in the publication of this program were:

Vice President and Publisher: Stanley J. Galek
Director of Production: Elizabeth Holthaus
Senior Assistant Editor: Sally Conover
Manufacturing Coordinator: Mary Beth Hennebury
Project Management, Design: Rollins Graphic Design and Production
Composition, Maps, Computer Art: Pre-Press Company, Inc.

Cover art: Michio Takayama, "Gate of Toledo," circa 1972–78

ISBN: 0-8384-2283-7
Manufactured in the United States of America.

Heinle & Heinle
An International Thomson Publishing Company
Boston, Massachusetts 02116 U.S.A.

15   04 03 02 01

To our parents, Charles McCloskey
and Greg and Marge Haran, with love
and appreciation.

The authors and publishers would like to acknowledge the contributions of the following individuals who reviewed and field-tested *Voices in Literature Bronze* at various stages of development and who offered many helpful insights and suggestions.

Reviewers

Yvette St. John
ESL Teacher, Portland (OR)

Lynn Slobodien
Balboa High School, San Francisco (CA)

Jean Bernard Johnston
Educational Insights, Amherst (MA)

Linda Sasser
Alhambra School District, Alhambra (CA)

Carolyn Bohlman
Maine Township High School, Parkridge (IL)

Janet Waters
University High School, Irvine (CA)

Field–testers

Jeff Morgenstein
Hudson High School, Hudson, Pasco County (FL)

Rick DeFranscisco
Newcomer Center, Woodside (CA)

Sharolyn Hutton
Newcomer Center, Ontario (CA)

Amy Perras
Paramount High School, Paramount (CA)

**Christine Skinner
Rio Mesa High School, Oxnard (CA)**

Greta Katen
Newcomer School, Fresno (CA)

Alex Gonzalez
South El Monte High School, South El Monte (CA)

Judy Page
Sanderson High School, Raleigh (NC)

**Elaine Kloetzly
Mansfeld Middle School, Tucson (AZ)**

Arlene Rotter
Newton County Schools, Covington, Georgia

Marge Boyle
Gwinnett County Schools, Lawrenceville, Georgia

Acknowledgments

We would like to thank our husbands, Jim Stack and Joel Reed, for their all-around support as treasure hunters, listeners, readers, and advice givers, and for their willingness to climb mountains and sleep in hammocks in the jungle to facilitate our collaboration. We are also grateful to our children, Erin, Deirdre, Sean, Kevin, and Tom, for their interest, patience, and understanding during our sometimes lengthy cross-continental trips and conversations.

We thank all our reviewers, piloters, and their students for their enthusiastic responses to the literature and activities in this book and for their constructive suggestions for improvement.

Scott Jackson provided invaluable help in creating the manuscript; we are most appreciative of his care and thoroughness.

Finally, we gratefully acknowledge Heinle & Heinle Publishers for listening to ESOL teachers and responding with the beautiful, accessible, and challenging series that our students need and deserve.

(continued on p. 199)

Welcome to *Voices in Literature Bronze*. This book was written for you, students from many cultures and language backgrounds. We hope it will help you learn English, learn to talk about literature, and explore themes that are found in many cultures. We hope that some of the selections will help you learn about other people and places. We also hope some will remind you of the experiences and stories of your families and friends.

Many of the activities in the book are meant to be done with other students. We hope you and your classmates will learn and discover new ideas from the text, your teacher, and each other. You will have choices to make and questions with more than one right answer. You will have a chance to write often and to do projects.

The first unit, *Patterns,* shows how patterns in English help you learn. In *Nature,* the second unit, you will study how writings from many cultures see the beauty and images of nature. Unit Three is about the many ways to send *Messages. People,* in all their variety, are the subject of Unit Four. The last unit, *Peace,* explores challenges to peace and the ways that young people can work to promote harmony among people and countries.

We hope you enjoy *Voices in Literature Bronze*. We would love to hear your ideas and opinions about it.

Mary Lou McCloskey
Lydia Stack

*V*oices in Literature Bronze provides teachers and students of English for speakers of other languages (ESOL) an anthology of high-quality literature. The selections and the activities for using those selections will help students interact with literature to benefit their language learning, to foster literary discussion, and to introduce to students the language and concepts of literature. A variety of ways for teachers and students to approach the literature selections, to interact with the actual texts, and to respond to the selections has been included.

Your students will come to the *Voices in Literature* series with varying exposure to literature and literary discussions. Therefore, we have chosen selections and created activities to suit the range of backgrounds of your multi-level class. Selections in the *Bronze* edition are authentic literature, but are often short and use predictable patterns to be accessible to newer learners of English.

Why use literature?

Literature is an appropriate, valuable, and valid medium to assist ESOL students in accomplishing important goals. Literature provides students with motivation to learn and models of high-quality language while it enhances students' imagination, interaction, and collaboration.

Motivation. Literature motivates students by touching on themes they care about, such as love, fear, communication, character, and hopes for a peaceful world in the future. Good literature is about the human experience; it is meaningful to students from different linguistic and cultural backgrounds.

Models. Carefully chosen literature provides models of high-quality language with sophistication and complexity appropriate to students' age levels. Literature offers new vocabulary in context and serves as a source for learning about the mechanics of language in authentic contexts, as they are used by masters of that language.

Imagination. Imagination is one of the abilities that make us fully human. Literature can give students the means to imagine and think creatively. Literature demands that the reader step into the author's world; good literature demands thought from the reader. Students who are learning a new language need and deserve the challenges to their imagination that appropriate literature provides.

Interaction and collaboration. Language is learned best in a setting in which it is put to use. Literature provides a common text from which students can negotiate meaning. Well-selected literature addresses issues that are vital to young readers and that stimulate lively discussion among students. Using literature in combination with collaborative activities helps students understand the literature better, relate it to their own ideas and experiences, and go beyond the literature to produce their own literature-related products.

What kinds of literature should be used?

In selecting texts for *Voices in Literature Bronze,* we have used a broad definition of literature and have included songs and poetry, fiction, nonfiction, drama, and folktales. We sought authentic and rich texts that provide high-quality language models. We feel that there is no need to "water down" the literature we use with ESOL students; we just need to choose it carefully. In making selections, we were also guided by the following concerns:

Student interest. Literature should be age-appropriate and should address themes of interest to the learners.

Linguistic accessibility. The language of the literature should be clear and simple enough for the student to understand, yet it must be expressive, figurative, and evocative to match the maturity and intellectual sophistication of the students. We have included, for example, many poetry selections. Songs and poetry are simple and memorable—often using rhyme, rhythm, and repetition to enhance comprehensibility—yet they are also complex, evoking deep emotion and thoughts in the reader.

Cultural relevance. Literature selected for ESOL students should reflect many cultures, address concerns of individuals who are experiencing cultural change, and teach about the new, English-speaking culture.

How can literature be used effectively in the ESOL classroom?

We have used a variety of strategies and structures to support students as they learn language through literature and study literature through language. Thematic organization offers students opportunities to relate concepts and works of literature to one another. The revisitation of themes, ideas, and terms provides enhanced context and thus improves comprehensibility. The supportive format we offer follows an "into-through-beyond" model that includes activities for use before, during, and after reading the literature.

Before you read. We use activities and discussion that connect students' own experience to the literary selection they will read and provide background information about the literature to guide them "into" the work.

The selection. We provide a variety of ways to guide students "through" the work, including activities such as reading aloud to students, shared reading, supportive questions during reading, dividing the reading into manageable "chunks," and many cooperative learning activities.

After you read. Finally, we use thought-provoking discussion questions, cooperative learning activities, experiences to expand comprehension of literary concepts and terms, writing activities, project ideas, and suggested further readings to take students "beyond" the work into their own high-level thinking and original creations. Many activities employ graphic organizers and learning strategies that can be adapted for use in other learning situations. At the end of each unit, we include activities to help students relate the works to one another around the unit themes.

At the end of the book we have included an alphabetic glossary of the vocabulary annotated in the text.

We hope that you and your students enjoy using the selections and activities in *Voices in Literature Bronze* and that they enrich your classroom learning community. We would love to hear from you and your students about your experiences with *Voices*.

Table of Contents

Unit 1: Patterns

Unit 3: Messages

Unit 4: People

Kocka Urvar by Victor de Vasarely, 1983

U N I T

Patterns

All languages use patterns.
Patterns make language easy
to remember. They also make
language fun to learn.

BEFORE YOU READ

➤ *Exploring Your Own Experience*

Find the Pattern (AM)

What comes next?

1, 2, 3, 4, __

ab cd ef __

/ . // . . /// . . . // . . . //// . . . .

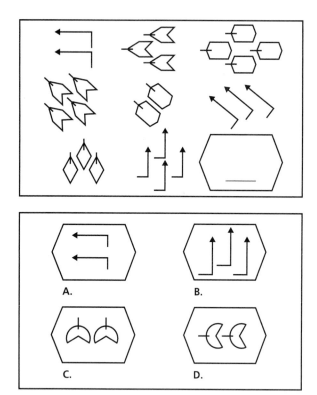

What comes next?

Draw a Picture

1. Find a picture in a book or magazine that shows what you like to do for fun on Saturday.
2. Show three classmates your picture.
3. Answer these questions about your picture:
   What are you doing?
   Who is with you?
   Where are you?
   What are you eating and drinking?
   What are you wearing?
4. Ask your classmates the questions about their pictures.

Students enjoying themselves at a Saturday night dance

➤ Background

This song comes from Nigeria.

Protesters in Nigeria

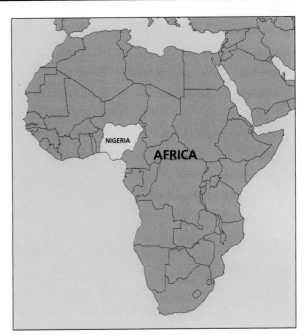

Nigeria, in the continent of Africa

These colorful characters are part of a Mardi Gras float in the New Orleans Mardi Gras parade.

Everybody Loves Saturday Night

Traditional

Everybody loves Saturday night.
Everybody loves Saturday night.
Everybody loves Saturday night.
Everybody loves Saturday night.
Everybody, everybody, everybody,
  everybody.
Everybody loves Saturday night.

Spanish
A todos les gusta la noche del sábado.

French
Tout le monde aime le samedi soir.

Chinese
Ren ren xi ai zhou liu zhi ye.

Armenian
Polores ge serenk shapat kisher.

Ebo (Nigerian)
Onye obula hura eke abali na anya.

➤ *Try This*

1. Tell the class about something you love or like very much.
2. Make new words to the song with things that many students love.
3. You can also make new words about things nobody likes.

I love pizza.

Kim and Maria love tacos.

Everybody loves weekends.

Nobody likes a rainy Sunday.

➤ *Learning About Language and Literature*

Chants AM

Chants are language patterns that you say aloud. Say these chants with your teacher.

> I love Saturday night.
> You love Saturday night.
> Kim loves Saturday night, too.
>
> We love Saturday night.
> You love Saturday night.
> They love Saturday night, too.

Days of the Week Chant

The chant below helps people remember the days of the week in English.

Solomon Grundy

Traditional

Solomon Grundy,
Born on Monday,
Grew up on Tuesday,
Married on **Wednesday,**
Got sick on **Thursday,**
Worse on **Friday,**
Died on **Saturday,**
Buried on **Sunday.**
This is the end
Of Solomon Grundy.

➤ *Writing*

Your Favorite Day AM

1. Draw a picture of your favorite day.
2. Label the parts of the picture.
3. Write in your journal about your picture.

A Chant AM

1. Write your own chant.
2. Use the patterns of "Everybody Loves Saturday Night."

I love Reggae.

You love Rock.

He loves Salsa.

You love Afropop.

We all love music.

➤ Exploring Your Own Experience

Your Favorite Music

1. Bring in your favorite tape or CD.

2. Play a favorite song for your classmates.

3. Show the class a favorite dance, or tell the class what the words of the song mean.

4. Ask your classmates questions about their music.

In Brazil, young people enjoy spending an evening of dancing and music.

➤ *Background*

The Inuit people live in Canada.

1. Look at the Inuit drummer in the picture on page 12. Imagine the sounds of Inuit drums.

2. Tell, draw, write, or show how you think the Inuit might dance to this music.

Inuit region of Canada.

Spring Dance by Napatchie Pootoogook, 1979

A Central Inuit Chant

Traditional

Ayii, ayii, ayii,
My arms, they wave high in the air,
My hands, they flutter behind my back,
They wave above my head
Like the wings of a bird.
Let me move my feet.
Let me dance.
Let me shrug my shoulders.
Let me shake my body.
Let me crouch down.
My arms, let me fold them.
Let me hold my hands under my chin.

wave   move back and forth
flutter   move fast up and down or side to side
shrug   move shoulders up
crouch   get down low
fold   lay one arm on top of another

AFTER YOU READ

➤ Try This

1. Work with a partner.
2. Read the poem to your partner.
3. Your partner acts out the movements.
4. Then you act out the poem while your partner reads.

➤ Learning About Language and Literature

Storyboards

People who make movies use storyboards to plan what will happen. A storyboard tells the story with pictures.

Below is a sample storyboard telling how to play a CD.

How to Play a CD (Compact Disc)

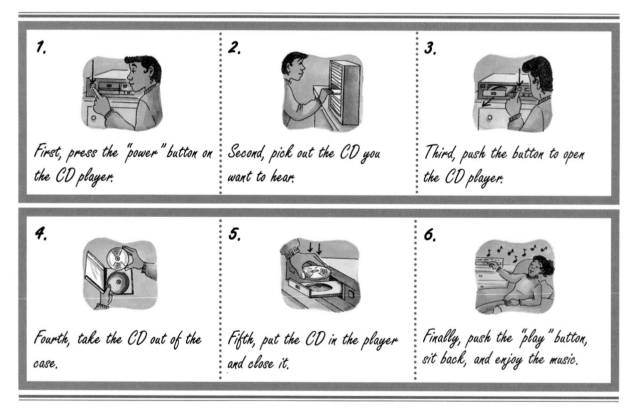

1. First, press the "power" button on the CD player.

2. Second, pick out the CD you want to hear.

3. Third, push the button to open the CD player.

4. Fourth, take the CD out of the case.

5. Fifth, put the CD in the player and close it.

6. Finally, push the "play" button, sit back, and enjoy the music.

➤ *Writing*

Writing with a Storyboard AM

You can use a storyboard to tell how to do something.

What can you teach someone to do?

1. Draw a storyboard.
2. Write the steps.
3. Teach someone.

Hints: Choose something simple, like making a sandwich. Add more squares to the storyboard if you need them.

Making a sandwich

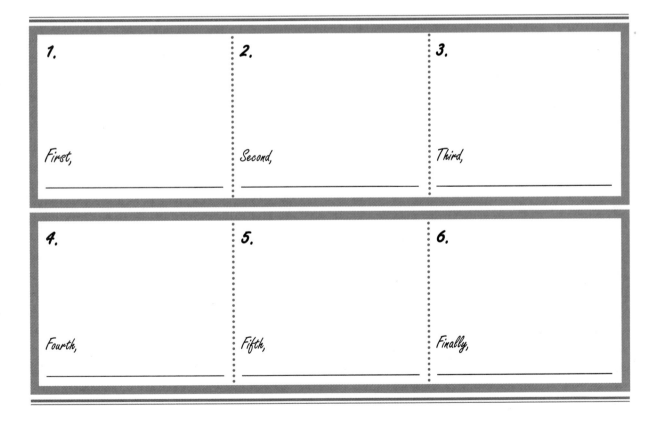

1.	2.	3.
First,	Second,	Third,
_____	_____	_____

4.	5.	6.
Fourth,	Fifth,	Finally,
_____	_____	_____

➤ *Exploring Your Own Experience*

Roundtable AM

The 365 days of the year are divided into 12 months. Share events in each month by using a "Roundtable."

1. Work with three other students.

2. Make a chart like the one below.

3. Pass the chart around the group.

4. Write something in one box of the chart each time it comes to you.

The Months			
Month	Name in Another Language	What I Think of	Picture or Symbol
January	enero	eating menudo on New Year's Day	
February			
March			
April			
May			
June			
July			
August			
September			
October			
November			
December			

➤ Background AM

1. Where were you born?
2. Find that country on the map of the world.
3. Find the place where you live now.
4. What is November like in both places?
5. What do you see in the sky in November? Does it snow?

What Do You See?

In the next poem, Anne Corkett describes what people from North America often see in November. Look at the shape of the poem. What do you see?

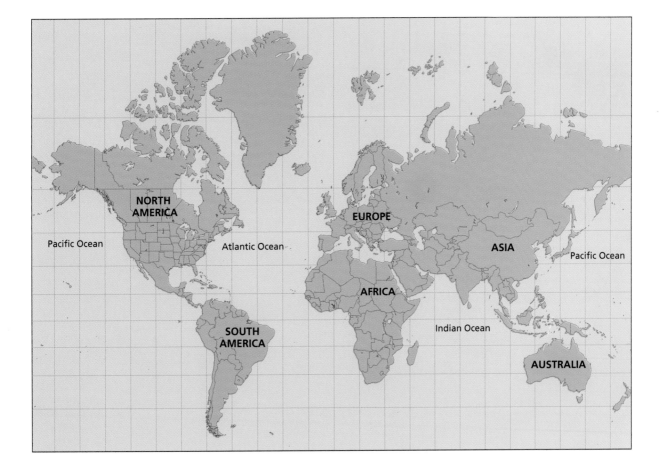

Day and Night by Maurits Escher, 1938

November

by Anne Corkett

sun
the
than
Snow   higher
and   fly
night   geese
comes   sky
down   of
into   ledge
the   yellow
last

➤ *Try This*

Seasons **AM**

The poem "November" describes a month of the year. November is in the fall season in North America.

In many places, there are four seasons in a year: summer, fall, winter, and spring.

In other places, there are two seasons: rainy and dry.

1. What are the seasons in the country where you were born?
2. Which months are in each season there?
3. Which months are in the seasons where you live now?
4. Show your answers on a chart.

A Useful Rhyme

English-speaking people have used the following rhyme for many, many years. It helps them remember how many days each month has. You may want to memorize this rhyme.

Thirty Days

Traditional

Thirty days has September
April, June, and November.
All the rest have thirty-one
Except February, which has twenty-eight
But in Leap Year, that's the time
When February has twenty-nine.

February						
S	M	T	W	T	F	S
					1	2	3
4	5	6	7	8	9	10
11	12	13	14	15	16	17
18	19	20	21	22	23	24
25	26	27	28			

January						
S	M	T	W	T	F	S
	1	2	3	4	5	6
7	8	9	10	11	12	13
14	15	16	17	18	19	20
21	22	23	24	25	26	27
28	29	30	31			

February						
S	M	T	W	T	F	S
				1	2	3
4	5	6	7	8	9	10
11	12	13	14	15	16	17
18	19	20	21	22	23	24
25	26	27	28	29		

March						
S	M	T	W	T	F	S
					1	2
3	4	5	6	7	8	9
10	11	12	13	14	15	16
17	18	19	20	21	22	23
$^{24}/_{31}$	25	26	27	28	29	30

April						
S	M	T	W	T	F	S
1	2	3	4	5	6	
7	8	9	10	11	12	13
14	15	16	17	18	19	20
21	22	23	24	25	26	27
28	29	30				

May						
S	M	T	W	T	F	S
		1	2	3	4	
5	6	7	8	9	10	11
12	13	14	15	16	17	18
19	20	21	22	23	24	25
26	27	28	29	30	31	

June						
S	M	T	W	T	F	S
						1
2	3	4	5	6	7	8
9	10	11	12	13	14	15
16	17	18	19	20	21	22
$^{23}/_{30}$	24	25	26	27	28	29

July						
S	M	T	W	T	F	S
	1	2	3	4	5	6
7	8	9	10	11	12	13
14	15	16	17	18	19	20
21	22	23	24	25	26	27
28	29	30	31			

August						
S	M	T	W	T	F	S
				1	2	3
4	5	6	7	8	9	10
11	12	13	14	15	16	17
18	19	20	21	22	23	24
25	26	27	28	29	30	31

September						
S	M	T	W	T	F	S
1	2	3	4	5	6	7
8	9	10	11	12	13	14
15	16	17	18	19	20	21
22	23	24	25	26	27	28
29	30					

October						
S	M	T	W	T	F	S
	1	2	3	4	5	
6	7	8	9	10	11	12
13	14	15	16	17	18	19
20	21	22	23	24	25	26
27	28	29	30	31		

November						
S	M	T	W	T	F	S
					1	2
3	4	5	6	7	8	9
10	11	12	13	14	15	16
17	18	19	20	21	22	23
24	25	26	27	28	29	30

December						
S	M	T	W	T	F	S
1	2	3	4	5	6	7
8	9	10	11	12	13	14
15	16	17	18	19	20	21
22	23	24	25	26	27	28
29	30	31				

➤ *Writing*

Your Favorite Month AM

1. Write about your favorite month.
2. Add a drawing, magazine pictures, or computer clip art.
3. You might choose to use this pattern:
   My favorite month is ____ because ____.

My favorite month is July because I go back to Mexico in July.

Shape Poems

"November" is a shape poem. The words of the poem are arranged in the shape of what the poem is about. "Concrete Cat" is also a shape poem.

Write your own shape poem.

1. Write the words.
2. Draw the shape in pencil.
3. Write the words on the shape.
4. Share it with classmates.

Concrete Cat

by Dorthi Charles

A   A
e   r   e   r

eYe   eYe   stripe stripe stripe stripes

whisker   whisker   stripe stripe stripe
whisker m   h whisker   stripe stripe stripe stripes   i l t a i l
         o   t   stripe stripe stripe
         U   stripe stripe stripe stripes

paw paw   paw paw   əsnoɯ

dishdish   litterbox
                              litterbox

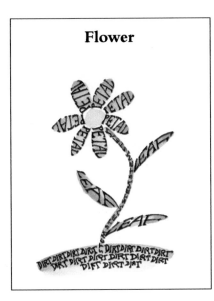

Flower

➤ Exploring Your Own Experience

What Is It For?

1. Find an interesting object in the classroom or bring one from home.
2. Get into a group of four.
3. Tell the group what your object is used for.

➤ Background

Play Concentration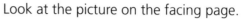

Look at the picture on the facing page.

1. Name as many of the objects as you can.
2. Find out the names of the others.
3. Play a game with a partner to learn the English words.

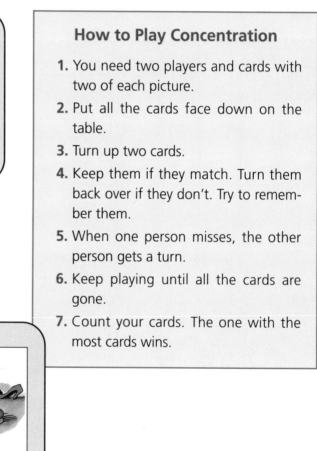

How to Play Concentration

1. You need two players and cards with two of each picture.
2. Put all the cards face down on the table.
3. Turn up two cards.
4. Keep them if they match. Turn them back over if they don't. Try to remember them.
5. When one person misses, the other person gets a turn.
6. Keep playing until all the cards are gone.
7. Count your cards. The one with the most cards wins.

The Artist's Room at Arles by Vincent Van Gogh, 1889

Trees Are for Climbing

by Dr. Fitzhugh Dodson

Trees are for climbing;
Words are for rhyming.
    Bikes are for riding,
    Bushes for hiding.
Blocks are for stacking,
Suitcases for packing.
    Clothes are for dressing,
    Riddles for guessing.
Bells are for clanging;
Drums are for banging.
    Stamps are for sticking,
    Ice cream for licking.
Shoes are for walking;
A voice is for talking.
    Tears are for weeping;
    A bed is for sleeping.
Milk is for drinking;
A brain is for thinking.

---

rhyming   using words ending with the same sound, like *cat* and *rat*
riddles   word puzzles to guess—for example, Q: "Why did the woman throw the butter out the window?" A: "To see a butterfly."

➤ *Try This*

Acting Out the Poem

1. With a partner, act out one line of the poem.
2. The class can guess which line you are acting out.

➤ *Learning About Language and Literature*

Questions and Answers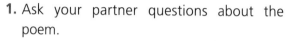

1. Ask your partner questions about the poem.
2. Answer your partner's questions.

> Q: What is a ____ for?
> A: A ____ is for _____.

> *Q: What are shoes for?*
>
> *A: Shoes are for walking.*

Shoes are for walking.

➤ *Writing*

What Is It For? (AM)

1. Work with three other students.
2. Write uses for the objects you and your classmates brought in.
3. Arrange your sentences in a poem.

Here are samples from other students. Do you agree?

Soft drinks are for drinking.

School is for thinking.

Glasses are for breaking.

Hands are for shaking.

Dishes are for washing.

Teeth are for brushing.

Radios are for playing.

Poems are for saying.

School is for learning English.

School is for making friends.

School is to make your parents happy.

School is for sleeping.

School is for playing ball after school.

School is for getting smart.

School is for a chance to be somebody.

➤ *Exploring Your Own Experience*

Four Corners AM

1. Why did you come to North America?

2. Go to the corner that best shows your reason.

3. Count the people in each corner, and make a graph.

4. Write about the graph.

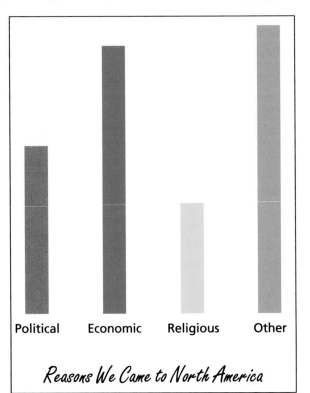

Reasons We Came to North America

➤ *Background*

People who moved to North America years ago
usually came to work on farms.

Next is the story of an immigrant family (a
family that moved to a new country). It is a
song sung by German Americans.

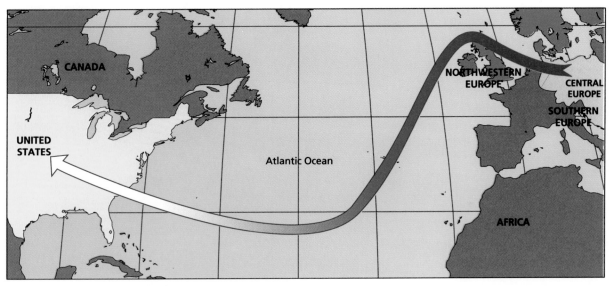

German immigrants traveled to North America many years ago.

Continuities by Romare Bearden, 1969

When I First Came to This Land

Traditional German American Folk Poem

When I first came to this land,
I was not a wealthy man.
I got myself a shack.
And I called that shack "Break My Back,"
And the land was sweet and good,
And I did what I could.

When I first came to this land,
I was not a wealthy man.
I got myself a farm.
And I called my farm "Muscle in My Arm,"
And I called my shack "Break My Back,"
And the land was sweet and good,
And I did what I could.

---

wealthy   rich
shack   small, old house

When I first came to this land,
I was not a wealthy man.
I got myself a wife.
And I called my wife "Love of My Life,"
And I called my farm "Muscle in My Arm,"
And I called my shack "Break My Back,"
And the land was sweet and good,
And I did what I could.

When I first came to this land,
I was not a wealthy man.
I got myself a cow.
And I called that cow "No Milk Now,"
And I called my wife "Love of My Life,"
And I called my farm "Muscle in My Arm,"
And I called my shack "Break My Back,"
And the land was sweet and good,
And I did what I could.

When I first came to this land,
I was not a wealthy man.
I got myself a son.
And I called that son "Lots of Fun,"
And I called that cow "No Milk Now,"
And I called my wife "Love of My Life,"
And I called my farm "Muscle in My Arm,"
And I called my shack "Break My Back,"
And the land was sweet and good,
And I did what I could.

When I first came to this land,
I was not a wealthy man.
I got myself a tree.
And I called that tree "Family Tree,"
And I called that son "Lots of Fun,"
And I called that cow "No Milk Now,"
And I called my wife "Love of My Life,"
And I called my farm "Muscle in My Arm,"
And I called my shack "Break my Back,"
And the land was sweet and good,
And I did what I could.

---

family tree   a picture of all the members of a family and their
relationships, in the shape of a tree

AFTER YOU READ

➤ *Try This*

Storyboard for a Line Story

"When I First Came to This Land" is a *line story*. Each time you tell the story or sing the song, you add a new line. Make a storyboard for the story.

1. Draw a storyboard for a line story like the one pictured below.
2. Fill in the events from "When I First Came to This Land," or tell your own story.
3. Use the map to retell the story to a partner.

➤ *Writing*

A Line Poem or Story

A line poem or story is one in which each new line adds something. Then all the other lines are repeated.

1. Make a new storyboard of a different story.
2. Write the story or poem.
3. You might like to use the pattern of "When I First Came to This Land." Repeat the story or poem, adding one new line each time.

1. When I first came to this land, I was not a wealthy man,	**2.** I got myself a farm.	**3.** And I called my farm "Muscle in My Arm,"
4. And I called my shack "Break My Back,"	**5.** _____ _____	**6.** _____ _____

➤ *Learning About Language and Literature*

Repetition (AM)

Repetition is the use of words, sounds, or phrases again and again.

Underline the new words in each *stanza* of "When I First Came to This Land." A stanza is a part or section of a poem.

Below, the new words in the second stanza are underlined.

And I called my farm "Muscle in My Arm,"

When I first came to this land,
I was not a wealthy man.
I got myself a <u>farm</u>.
And I called my farm "<u>Muscle</u> in <u>My</u> <u>Arm</u>,"
And I called my shack "Break My Back,"
And the land was sweet and good,
And I did what I could.

What is repeated in this poem?

Unit Follow-Up

➤ Making Connections

Unit Project Ideas

Here are some possible unit projects. Use things you learned in the unit in your project. If you want, choose a project of your own and check it out with your teacher.

1. Action Word Wheel Game. (AM) Action words tell what someone or something does. They are also called *verbs.* Action words from "Solomon Grundy" are *born, grew up,* and *married.* Can you find others?

- Collect interesting action words from this unit.
- Write them on a word wheel like the one in the picture.
- Practice the words with a partner.

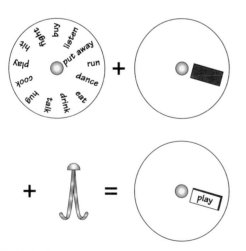

Word Wheel

2. Pattern Hunt. (AM)

- Choose a favorite word pattern from the selections in this unit—for example, "Everybody loves _____" or "A _____ is for _____."
- Ask ten other students to complete the pattern.
- Arrange the answers as a poem, or illustrate them with drawings or pictures cut from magazines. Make a book with the poem and the pictures.

3. Storyboard. (AM) Use a storyboard to illustrate and tell about something that happened in your life.

- Make a storyboard of what happened to you.
- Label the pictures.
- Tell your story aloud for about one minute as someone audiotapes or videotapes you.
- Watch or listen to the tape to see how your speaking is improving.
- Keep your tape to compare with other tapes you make later.

36 Unit 1: *Patterns*

4. Time Mobile. A mobile is an artwork with hanging, moving parts. Some artists, like Alexander Calder, are famous for their mobiles. Make a mobile to hang in your room that displays months of the year, days of the week, seasons, numbers, or another pattern that you want to learn.

- Cut out shapes to represent the days (or whichever pattern you've chosen).
- Write the names on each shape in beautiful letters, and decorate them.
- Hang the shapes from coat hangers on threads of different lengths.

Untitled by Alexander Calder, 1976

5. Song or Poem Search.

- Find other songs or poems that have patterns like the ones in this unit.
- Bring in a recording or write out the *lyrics* (words of a song) to share with the class.
- What does the song or poem mean to you? Tell the class.

6. New Words Dictionary.

- Start a dictionary of words that you want to learn.
- Use a spiral notebook.
- Write one letter of the alphabet at the top of each page.
- When you find a new word you want to remember, write it on the page with that word's first letter at the top.
- Write and/or draw the meaning of your word.

7. Word Database. **AM** A database is a place to keep organized facts. You can make a database on a chart or with a computer.

To make a word database:
- Collect new words that you have learned during this unit.
- Plan the information you want.

- Make up *fields* (special places for facts) for:
  The word.
  The meaning of the word.
  A picture or symbol to represent the word.
  The word in a sentence.
  How to pronounce the word. (optional)
  What kind of word it is (noun, verb, adjective, etc.). (optional)

Word Database

Word	Meaning	Sentence	Picture or Symbol	Type
riddle	word puzzle for guessing	"What is black and white and **read** all over?" is a riddle.	What is black and white and read all over?	noun

Further Reading (AM)

Following are some materials related to this unit that you might enjoy.

• ***And the Green Grass Grew All Around: Folk Poetry from Everyone,*** collected by Alvin Schwartz. New York: HarperCollins,1992. Folk poetry is poetry that people everywhere make up and pass on to others. This book includes great songs and poems about people, school, fun, and many other topics. Many of the folk poems are funny.

• ***Chicken Soup with Rice,*** by Maurice Sendak. New York: Harper and Row, 1962. Sendak tells us what to do during each month of the year — and it always has something to do with chicken soup with rice. "I told you once/I told you twice/all seasons of the year are nice/for eating chicken soup with rice!"

• ***Rise Up Singing: The Group-Singing Song Book,*** edited by Peter Blood-Patterson. Bethlehem, PA: Sing Out Corporation, 1988. This book includes the words and chords to 1,200 songs! A favorite "line story" song is "The Old Woman Who Swallowed a Fly" (p. 171).

• ***Talking to the Sun: An Illustrated Anthology of Poems for Young People,*** selected by Kenneth Koch and Kate Farrell. New York: Holt, Rinehart and Winston, 1985. This book has great poetry and great art, in categories like "All the Pretty Little Horses" and "A Rabbit as King of the Ghosts." The book includes some excellent concrete or "shape" poems.

• ***'Til All the Stars Have Fallen,*** selections by David Booth. New York: Viking Penguin, 1989. David Booth, an education professor from Toronto, has collected (mostly) Canadian poems from many cultures, including some concrete or "shape" poems.

• ***Very Last First Time,*** by Jan Andrews. Buffalo, NY: Groundwood Books, 1985. This story takes place in a present-day Inuit community. When the tide is out in the winter, the Inuit people make holes in the ice and go under the ice to hunt for mussels. Part of growing up is doing this alone for the first time.

• ***Where the Sidewalk Ends,*** poems and drawings by Shel Silverstein. New York: Harper and Row, 1974. Shel Silverstein never grew up. His poems and drawings are full of fun and silliness and thoughts about life from the point of view of young people.

A butterfly clings to a flower in the early-morning dew.

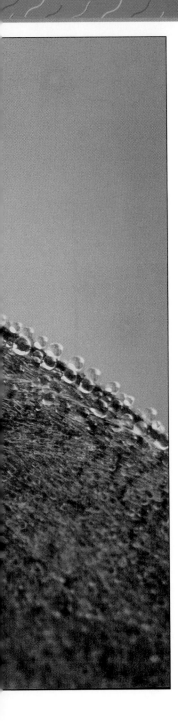

UNIT

2

Nature

Nature gives us many ideas
and images to read, write,
and talk about. We need to
take time to study and enjoy
nature.

➤ *Exploring Your Own Experience*

Nature Watch (AM)

1. Sit alone outside to observe nature.
2. Make a sense chart like the one on the right.
3. Write down what you see, hear, feel, and smell in nature.
4. In the classroom, share and discuss with three other students what you observed.
5. Make a list of things you observed and how many people saw them.

Sense Chart
What do you see?
What do you hear?
What do you feel?
What do you smell?

➤ *Background*

The Taos Pueblo Indians

The author of the following poem likes to write about the Taos Pueblos. The Taos Pueblos are a group of Native Americans who live in the state of New Mexico. They have a strong spirit and are close to nature.

A clear blue New Mexico sky lends a beautiful backdrop to this Pueblo village home.

Robed Journey of the Rainbow Clan by Helen Hardin, 1976

Three Sisters

by Nancy Wood

We are the Three Sisters of Fire and
Earth and Water.
Without us, nothing lives or grows.

We are the Three Daughters of Sun and
Moon and Stars.
Without us, no path exists through the
universe.

We are the Three Wives of Birds and
Trees and Animals.
Without us, there would be no wings or
roots or bones.

We are the Three Mothers of Clouds and
Wind and Rain.
Without us, our children would go
hungry.

---

exists   is
universe   all that there is

We are the Three Friends of Beauty.
Without us, flowers would look like
      stones.

We are the Three Grandmothers of
      Wisdom.
Without us, men would only speak of
      war.

We are the Three Aunts of
      Endurance.
Without us, what would survive?

---

wisdom   great knowledge and good judgment
endurance   the ability to be strong and last for a
     long time
survive   stay alive

ABOUT THE AUTHOR

Nancy Wood is a poet, novelist, and photographer. She has won many awards for her work. Ms. Wood lives in Santa Fe, New Mexico. There she enjoys the wilderness of the southwestern United States. For many years, Native Americans have been her friends and teachers.

➤ **Nancy Wood (born 1936)** ◄

AFTER YOU READ

▶ *Learning About Language and Literature*

Voice

Voice is the person who is speaking in a poem. Sometimes the person who is speaking in a poem is not the poet. Then we say that the poet is writing in another "voice."

1. Who is speaking in this poem?
2. How would this poem be different if the sisters were not speaking? It might begin like this:

> *They are the Three Sisters of Fire and Earth and Water.*
>
> *Without them, nothing lives or grows.*

3. What if the poet were speaking to the sisters? It might begin like this:

> *You are the Three Sisters of Fire and Earth and Water.*
>
> *Without you, nothing lives or grows.*

4. Change the *voice,* or speaker, in other lines of the poem.
5. Discuss: Which voice do you like best? Why?

What Comes in Threes?

The poem is called "Three Sisters." How do you think the number "three" is important?

1. Reread the poem.
2. Find anything else that comes in a group of three.
3. List the things you find on a chart like the one below.
4. Share your list with your class.
5. What other things in nature come in threes?

What Comes in Threes?	
Three Sisters	*fire, earth, and water*

➤ Try This

Making a Mandala AM

A *mandala* is a symbol of the universe. It is a design in a circle shape.

1. Work in groups of three or four.
2. Use a large sheet of paper.
3. Draw a mandala with two parts.
4. One part shows what the world is like with the sisters. The other shows what the world is like without the sisters.

➤ Writing

Write About Your Mandala

Make a new mandala that shows two sides of yourself. Then write about it.

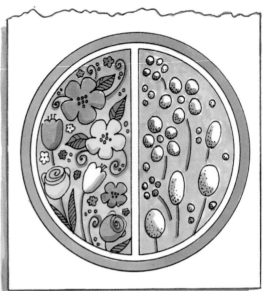

➤ *Exploring Your Own Experience*

Weather Metaphors

North Americans describe a heavy rain by saying, "It's raining cats and dogs" or "It's pouring."

1. Think about other ways that people tell about weather in English or in other languages.

2. Share these ways with your class.

3. Draw a picture of one of the ways people talk about weather.

4. Post the picture in your classroom.

5. Tell a small group of students about your picture.

➤ *Background*

Weather Words

We use many different words to talk about wet weather. When it rains only a little, we call it a "drizzle" or "mist." The biggest storms, with very strong winds and very heavy rain, we call hurricanes. Hurricanes can destroy houses, trees, or anything else in their way. The next two poems are about two kinds of wet weather.

Squall at the Large Bridge, Ohashi by Ando Hiroshige, 1857

Rain

by Dionne Brand

It finally came,
it beat on the house
it bounced on the flowers
it banged the tin roof
it rolled in the gutters
it made the street muddy
it spilled on the village
it licked all the windows
it jumped on the hill.
It stayed for two days
and then it left.

beat   hit hard, like you hit a drum
bounced   jumped back, as when you
throw a ball against something
gutters   U-shaped pipes on the edge
of a roof to help the rain run off the
roof
spilled   emptied out, as in "spilled
milk"

Hurricane

by Dionne Brand

Shut the windows
Bolt the doors
Big rain coming
Climbing up the mountain.

Neighbors whisper
Dark clouds gather
Big rain coming
Climbing up the mountain.

Gather in the clotheslines
Pull down the blinds
Big wind rising
Coming up the mountain.

---

bolt   lock

whisper   talk in a very soft voice

gather   come together

clotheslines   ropes for hanging clothes to dry

blinds   window coverings made of many metal pieces
that open and close

rising   moving upward toward the sky

Branches falling
Raindrops flying
Tree tops swaying
People running
Big wind blowing
Hurricane! on the mountain.

....

swaying   moving back and forth

ABOUT THE AUTHOR

Dionne Brand was born in Trinidad and later immigrated to Toronto. She has been called, "one of the best young poets writing in Canada today." Brand also writes fiction and non-fiction. She identifies with the struggles of Carribean people both in her homeland and in immigrant communities of Canada.

➤ **Dionne Brand (born 1953)** ◄

➤ *Try This*

Word Squares AM

1. Make Word Squares to study new words.
2. Choose difficult words from the poems above.
3. Add other words you need to know.

Word Square	
Word: love	**Sentence:** I love my mother.
Meaning: a strong feeling of caring for someone else	**Symbol:**

Shape Poems

You can also remember words by making them into shape poems like those in Unit 1. Try to make a shape poem with one of your difficult words. Below are shape poems that other students made.

➤ *Learning About Language and Literature*

Bringing Things to Life (AM)

In "Rain," the poet speaks about rain as if it were alive. She writes, for example,

> *it licked all the windows*
> *it jumped on the hill.*

1. What animals or people act that way?
2. Find more examples of poems that show weather acting like people or animals.
3. Share the lines of poetry you find with your classmates.

How Poets Show Feelings or Emotions

In "Hurricane," the poet shows the excitement and danger of the moment before a hurricane in several ways.

1. She uses short sentences, as if people are in a hurry.
2. She gives orders to prepare for the storm.

Can you find other examples of these ways of using words? Are there other ways that she tells the reader to hurry?

AFTER YOU READ

➤ *Writing*

Writing a Weather Poem (AM)

You have already seen different kinds of poems. A poem with five lines is called a *cinquain*. Each line uses certain kinds of words. Write a cinquain about an experience you have had with bad weather (or another topic you choose). Share your writing with a classmate.

Here is the form:

Line 1: a noun (person, place, or thing)

Line 2: two words that tell about the noun

Line 3: three *-ing* words that show action about the noun

Line 4: one four-word phrase or sentence about the noun

Line 5: the noun again (or a word that means the same)

Blizzard
White world
Snowing, blowing, freezing
Lost in empty space
Blizzard

➤ Exploring Your Own Experience

Do a Quickwrite AM

Can you remember seeing or hearing something in nature that surprised you? Did you want to remember that moment forever? Was it a sunset? A rabbit eating clover in your backyard? A cactus blooming?

1. Write about one moment in nature that you remember very well.

2. Write without stopping for a few minutes.

3. Try to write your ideas down. Don't worry about correctness right now.

4. Share your ideas with a classmate.

➤ Background

Haiku are short poems about nature. Long ago, the Japanese invented this kind of poem. Haiku, like other poems, can often be understood in more than one way.

Man Chasing a Hat on a Windy Day by unknown Japanese artist (date unknown)

Spring by Aya Itagaki, 1992

Three Haiku

Coming from the woods
A bull has a lilac sprig
Dangling from a horn

—Richard Wright

---

lilac   North American shrub with sweet-smelling lavender (pale purple)
or white flowers in the spring
sprig   very small branch with leaves
dangling   hanging, almost ready to fall off

At dawn
The pink clouds,
Like hundreds of crabs,
Creep from the hollows of heaven.

—Akiko Yosano

Clouds' Duet by Aya Itagaki, 1995

crabs   sea creatures with claws and round shells
creep   move very slowly, crawl like a baby
hollows   shallow holes or depressions in the ground

Evening Shower by Aya Itagaki, 1995

Come on, Owl!
Come on, change that look of yours
Now in the soft spring rain!

—Issa

Richard Wright wrote about the difficult experiences of African Americans in the United States. He wrote a novel about racial conflicts in inner-city Chicago and an autobiography written in the form of a novel. He was born in Mississippi and later lived in Chicago, New York, and Paris.

➤ **Richard Wright (1908–1960)** ◄

Akiko Yosano, Japanese poet and literary critic, became famous for the original flair of her poetry. She founded and taught at a school for girls, and she worked to translate a classic text from 11th-century Japan into modern Japanese.

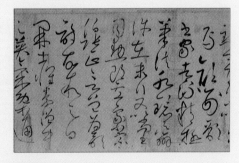

➤ **Akiko Yosano (1878–1942)** ◄

Issa (the pen name for Kobayashi Yataro) wrote poems in a simple style dealing with the everyday lives of Japanese people. His sympathy for the loneliness and struggles of ordinary people grew out of difficulties he experienced in his personal life.

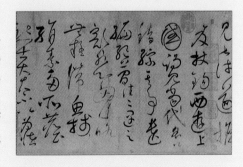

➤ **Issa (1763–1828)** ◄

➤ *Try This*

Counting Syllables

A syllable is a part of a word. *Na·ture* has two syllables. *Rain* has one syllable. Haiku usually have seventeen syllables. They are sometimes arranged in three lines like this:

First line: five syllables
Second line: seven syllables
Third line: five syllables

Count the syllables in each line of the haiku on page 60. How many syllables are in each line? What are the patterns you find?

➤ *Learning About Language and Literature*

Contrast AM

Poets often use *contrast* to compare two people or things that are very different. Can you find two very different things or animals that are contrasted in each of the three haiku on page 60? Does the description make you think of something else? Try to fill in a chart like the one below with your answers. Discuss them with your class.

Com-ing from the woods	5 syllables
A bull has a li-lac sprig	7 syllables
Dang-ling from a horn	5 syllables

Elements of Haiku		
Author	Two Things Contrasted	Makes me think of . . .
Richard Wright	bull, lilacs	war and peace

➤ *Writing*

Brainstorm

To develop a list of words for writing haiku, *brainstorm*.

1. Look at pictures of the seasons for inspiration.
2. Review your quickwrite for ideas for nature poems.
3. With classmates, write words about your nature topics on self-stick notes.
4. Put the words into categories.

Write Haiku

> black velvet sky
>
> stars blue crystals on water
>
> I look in your eyes

1. Use the self-stick notes to help you write short poems about nature.
2. Share your poems with classmates.
3. Revise your poems and illustrate them with drawings or magazine pictures.
4. Post them in the classroom or publish them as a class book.

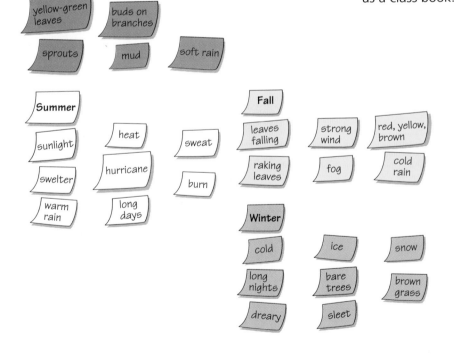

Spring

yellow-green leaves — buds on branches

sprouts — mud — soft rain

Summer

sunlight — heat — sweat

swelter — hurricane — burn

warm rain — long days

Fall

leaves falling — strong wind — red, yellow, brown

raking leaves — fog — cold rain

Winter

cold — ice — snow

long nights — bare trees — brown grass

dreary — sleet

➤ *Exploring Your Own Experience*

Listen to Silence: Cluster Map (AM)

1. Close your eyes and listen while everyone is quiet for three minutes.

2. Talk with a partner about the things you heard.

3. With your classmates, make a cluster map like the one below. Show what you heard.

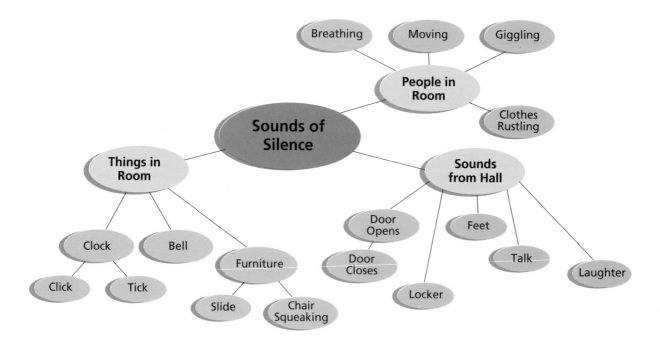

➤ *Background*

Sacred Corn

Sacred means "holy" or "very special." Corn was a sacred food for some native people of North America. In an Aztec legend, Quetzalcoatl (ket sal ko ot l), god of agriculture, first discovered corn in the crack of a rock.

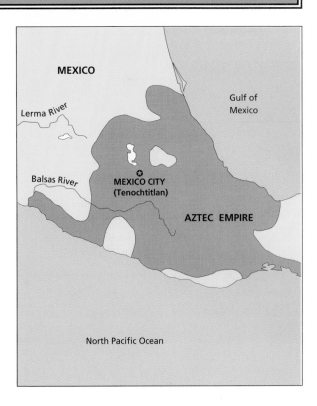

An image of the god Quetzalcoatl, the "plumed serpent" of ancient Mexican culture, as seen at Teotihuacán, Mexico

Ear-of-corn

an Ancient Aztec Poem

Ear-of-corn
you are a copper bell
you are a fruit pit
you are a sea shell
   white
you are crystal
   white

you are a green stone
you are a bracelet
you are precious
you are our flesh
you are our bones

---

copper reddish-colored metal

Prayers of a Blue Corn Mother by Helen Hardin, 1974

The Other Way to Listen

by Byrd Baylor

I used to know
an old man
who could
walk
by any
cornfield
and hear
the corn
singing.

"Teach me,"
I'd say
when we'd
passed on by.
(I never said
a word
while he was listening.)

"Just tell me
how
you learned
to hear
that
corn."

And he'd say,
"It takes
a lot of
practice.
You can't
be
in a hurry."

And I'd say,
"I have
the time."

He was so
good
at listening —
once
he heard
wildflower seeds
burst open,
beginning
to grow
underground.

That's hard to do.

He said
he was just
lucky
to have been
by himself
up there
in the canyon
after a rain.

....

canyon   a place where a river has made a deep cut in
the earth

He said
it was the quietest place
he'd ever been
and he stayed there
long enough to
understand
the quiet.

I said,
"I bet you were
surprised
when you heard
those seeds."

But
he said,
"No,
I wasn't surprised at all.
It seemed like the most
natural
thing
in the world."

He just smiled,
remembering.

The author of "Ear-of-corn" is unknown, or *anonymous*. We do know, however, that Aztec poems were written in picture books now called *codices*. Codices were about sixteen feet long. They were folded so that they could be opened like a screen.

➤ **Ancient Aztecs** ◄

Byrd Baylor, author of "The Other Way to Listen," grew up in the deserts of the southwestern United States. Her poems tell about her love for nature and the Southwest.

➤ **Byrd Baylor (born 1924)** ◄

➤ *Learning About Language and Literature*

Dialogue

Dialogue is when a writer uses the actual words of speakers. Byrd Baylor's poem uses dialogue. She tells the story of how a man taught the speaker in the poem to listen.

1. How can you tell when someone is speaking?

2. How can you tell when the speaker changes?

3. Find where the author uses quotation marks (" ") around a person's speech.

A Special Kind of Poem

An *ode* is a poem that praises something. Often the poet speaks to the thing being praised. "Ear-of-corn" is like an ode. The poet praises the ear of corn by calling it other things. What are some of the things that the poet calls the ear of corn?

➤ *Try This*

Comparing Things in Poetry

In "Ear-of-corn," the speaker talks to the corn. The speaker tells the corn that it is many things.

1. Name the things the poet compares to corn.

2. Tell how each thing is like corn.

3. Use a chart like the one below.

Things Compared to Corn	How They Are Like Corn
copper bell	valuable, brown silk is copper-colored
fruit pit	
sea shell—white	

Writing Dialogue

1. Talk to a small group of classmates about something you like to do.
2. Record your conversation.
3. Try writing down the words of two speakers from a short part of your tape.
4. See the example below.

> "Teach me," I'd say,
> when we'd passed on by.
> (I never said a word
> while he was listening.)
>
> "Just tell me
> how you learned to hear that corn."
>
> And he'd say, "It takes
> a lot of practice.
> You can't be in a hurry."

➤ Writing

Try one of the following.

Writing Quotations

Write a short poem or story using dialogue.

Writing an Ode

Write a short poem to praise something you like very much. You can use the pattern of the Aztec poem "Ear-of-corn."

> ### Rollerblades-of-mine
>
> Rollerblades-of-mine.
>
> You are a magic carpet.
>
> You are a fast car.
>
> You are the prison keys.
>
> You are a summer vacation.
>
> You are a sunny day.
>
> You are rocky road ice cream.
>
> You are mine and fine.

➤ *Exploring Your Own Experience*

Know/Want to Know/Learn Chart (K/W/L Chart) AM

1. Work in a small group.

2. Use a chart like the one below.

3. In the first column, write down everything you know about rainforests.

4. In the second column, write down everything you want to know about rainforests.

5. Share your ideas with the class. Make a class chart.

Know/Want to Know/Learned Chart		
K	*W*	*L*
There's a lot of rain.	What kinds of plants grow there?	
Lots of animals live there.	What kinds of animals live there?	
	Why are they important?	

➤ Background

What Is a Rainforest? AM

Look at the chart below. It includes some basic information about rainforests.

1. Work with a partner.
2. Each partner covers one side of his or her chart.
3. One partner reads a question. The other partner guesses which answer goes with it.
4. The other partner reads an answer, and the first partner tries to guess which question goes with it.
5. Take turns until both of you know the answers to all the questions.

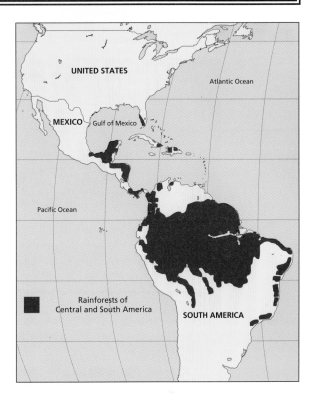

Rainforest Information	
Where are the rainforests?	Near the equator
How much rainfall is there in a year in a rainforest?	About 400 inches (1,024 cm) a year
What is the average temperature?	Average temperature is 80 degrees Fahrenheit (27 degrees Celsius)
How many seasons are there each year?	One season
What kinds of trees are there?	Most trees are evergreen.
How many different kinds are there?	There are more than 750 kinds of trees.

Rainforest, Victoria, Australia

Saving the Rainforests

What would the world be like without trees? To find out, just hold your breath. Tropical rainforests are the "lungs" of the Earth. They take carbon dioxide out of the air and give off oxygen for us to breathe. They also help keep the earth's temperature down.

But people are destroying the rainforests. They are cutting down trees in order to survive.

Most rainforests are located in countries with little industry and growing populations. Cutting down trees is a way to make room for farms. The governments in those countries and companies from other countries also cut down trees for lumber and cattle ranches. Lumber, beef, and other products are then sold in the U.S. and other countries.

---

lungs   body organs in your chest that help you breathe
carbon dioxide   waste gas from mammals' breathing, necessary gas for plants
oxygen   gas needed for plants and animals to live
destroying   ruining, making no good
survive   continue to live
located   found
industry   making of goods, manufacturing

But when a rainforest is destroyed, all the plants and animals that live there are destroyed, too. And the Earth will heat up if there aren't enough trees to take carbon dioxide out of the air. Scientists call this *global warming*. It's a serious world problem.

What can be done? Can people survive without cutting down their rainforests? Many say yes—but it will take a lot of planning and work with other countries. The survival of the planet depends on it.

---

destroyed   ruined, wrecked, made no good

AFTER YOU READ

➤ *Try This*

Venn Diagram

Compare where you live with the rainforest. Use a Venn diagram like the one below.

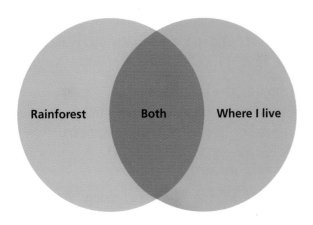

➤ *Learning About Language and Literature*

Using the Library

Look back over your K/W/L chart (page 76).

1. What did you learn from reading the article? Think and discuss.
2. Write these things in the "learn" column.
3. What do you still want to learn? Think and discuss.
4. Go to the library to find your answers.
5. Ask the librarian to help you.

➤ *Writing*

What Did You Learn?

In your journal, write about what you learned about rainforests. Then try one of the following activities, or think of your own activity to share what you learned about the rainforests.

1. Write a list of things people can do to help save the rainforests.
2. Write a letter to an environmental organization. Ask for information on rainforests.
3. Write a song about the rainforests. One class used the tune of the folk song "And the Green Grass Grew All Around." Their song was called "And the Green Trees Grew All Around and Around."

Unit Follow-Up

➤ *Making Connections*

Unit Project Ideas

Here are some possible unit projects. Use things you learned in the unit in your project. You may also choose to think up a project of your own. Be sure to tell your teacher about your project.

1. Nature Collage.

- Work with a group of students.
- Choose a place.
- Each person studies some plant or animal that lives there.
- Draw, paint, or make a paper cutout of your plant or animal.
- Write a sentence telling about it.
- Put everyone's artwork and sentences together on a large sheet of mural paper.
- Tell your class about your project.

2. Where Would You Like to Visit? Is there some beautiful place in nature that you would like to visit?

- Find pictures of this place.
- Write about it, telling why you want to go there.

3. Saving the Rainforests.

- Go to the library to study things that we can do to help save the rainforests.
- Make a chart of ten things that you and your classmates can do.
- Visit another class or group. Tell them about your ten ideas.

4. Write a Letter. AM

- Write a letter to someone in the government. Tell what you want this person to do to protect our natural environment.
- Work with your teacher and classmates to edit the letter.
- Send the final copy to the government representative.

5. Comparing Views of Nature. AM

- Choose two of your favorite selections from the unit.
- Use a Venn diagram to compare and contrast the views of nature in these two pieces.
- Compare your Venn diagram with someone else's.

Further Reading (AM)

Following are some materials related to this unit that you might enjoy.

• *FernGully: The Last Rainforest.* Beverly Hills, CA: Fox Video, 1992. In this highly acclaimed fantasy film, an employee of a company that is cutting down the rainforest is changed by magical events. He works to overcome the evil power that's destroying the rainforest.

• *Grandfather's Dream,* by Holly Keller. New York: Greenwillow Books, 1994. This book tells how a village in Vietnam successfully dammed part of the Mekong Delta so that the beautiful Sarus cranes could roost in the area.

• *In a Spring Garden,* edited by Richard Lewis. New York: Dial, 1989. A delightful selection of spring haiku is illustrated with watercolor and collage by award-winning artist Ezra Jack Keats.

• *The Native Stories from Keepers of the Earth,* by Michael J. Caduto and Joseph Bruchac. Los Angeles: First House Publisher, 1991. These 24 stories, collected from various Native North American groups, deal with the relationship of people to the earth. These stories can help us learn how to live with other creatures in harmony with nature.

• *The People Who Hugged the Trees,* Deborah Lee Rose. Niwat, CO: Roberts Rinehart, 1992. In this story from the state of Rajasthan in India, villagers hold a "sit-in" to stop a ruler from cutting down trees to build a new palace. The village relies on the grove of trees to protect it from desert storms.

• *Rain Forest,* by Helen Cowcher. New York: Farrar, Straus and Giroux, 1988. This book describes how the needs of animals living in the rainforests clash with what humans want. Machines cutting down the rainforests have threatened the centuries-old peaceful existence of the native plants and animals.

• *Tropical Rain Forest.* Philadelphia: Coronet, 1989. This short video explores the many kinds of life in the tropical rainforest. Each layer of the forest provides its own separate habitat for plants and animals.

• *Welcome Back, Sun,* by Michael Emberley. New York: Little, Brown, 1993. A girl and her family who live in the mountains of Norway make their yearly walk up Mount Gusta to see the first rays of the sun in the spring.

• *The Year of the Panda,* by Miriam Schlein. New York: HarperCollins, 1992. This is the story of a Chinese boy who discovers a sick, abandoned panda bear. The boy seeks the help of a scientist from the United States to learn more about endangered species.

Petroglyphs in Lewis Canyon, Val-Verde County, Texas

Messages

What are some powerful ways to send messages? What kinds of messages have you sent lately? Unit Three explores ways that people use words, pictures, and sounds to send messages to one another. See how many different ways you can find to send messages.

➤ *Exploring Your Own Experience*

Brainstorm (AM)

Think of all the ways you see people send and receive messages every day. With your class, see how long a list you can make.

Message			
Sender	Receiver	Mode	Purpose
Mom	Doctor	phone	make appointment
Minh	Maria	note	find out if there's play practice

➤ Background

Do people in your family leave notes and messages for each other? The poem on page 89 seems like a message that someone might find on a refrigerator one morning.

Plums by Charles Demuth, 1925

This Is Just to Say

by William Carlos Williams

I have eaten
the plums
that were in
the icebox

and which
you were probably
saving
for breakfast

Forgive me
they were delicious
so sweet
and so cold

----

icebox   refrigerator
delicious   having a very good taste

William Carlos Williams was the son of an English father and a Puerto Rican mother. He was a medical doctor as well  as a writer of poetry, novels, and plays. He wrote about his every-day experiences and people he knew.

➤ **William Carlos Williams (1883–1963)** ◄

➤ *What Do You Think?*

1. What is the purpose of the poem?
2. What did the speaker do wrong?
3. Is the speaker really sorry?
4. Would you forgive the speaker? Why or why not?

➤ *Try This*

Walking Gallery

1. Work in groups of four.
2. In your group, draw a picture of what you see when you read or hear the poem.
3. Important! Take turns—each person must draw some part of the picture.
4. Put the group pictures on the wall.
5. Tell the other groups about your picture. Each person in your group should say something about the picture.

➤ Learning About Language and Literature

How Are Poems Different from Other Kinds of Writing?

There are many kinds of poems. Poems can tell stories or describe feelings or things that happen. How are poems different from other kinds of writing? One difference is how they look on the page.

Compare page 51 (a poem) with pages 79–80 (prose, or writing that is not poetry). How do the pages look different?

➤ Writing

Class Book of Excuses AM

"This Is Just to Say" is an apology or excuse that the speaker offers for doing something she or he shouldn't have done. Try writing your own excuse for something you did.

1. With a partner, write a one-sentence excuse or apology.
2. Rewrite it in big letters on a large strip of paper.
3. Put everyone's strip on the wall.
4. Arrange the lines so that they sound like a poem.
5. Think up a good title for the poem/book.
6. Illustrate the lines and put the final poem up in the classroom, or make a class book.

Sorry I missed you last night. I had to wash my hair.

I'm sorry I don't have my homework. The dog ate it.

I apologize for not paying attention. I'm in love.

I'm sorry I ruined your watch. I wanted to see if it was waterproof.

➤ *Exploring Your Own Experience*

Think–Pair–Share

Think about a time when someone told you a secret.

1. *Think.* Think about that time. Who was it? What happened? How did you feel?

2. *Pair.* Share your thoughts with a partner. (You don't have to share the secret!)

3. *Share.* Get together with another pair of students. Take turns talking. Each person tells what his or her partner shared.

Students sharing a secret

➤ *Background*

What Is a Diary?

A diary is a book in which people write about their thoughts and their lives. Some people don't let anyone else read their diaries. Brainstorm about things people could write in a diary.

My Diary

by Bernard Waber

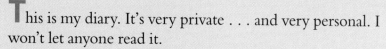

This is my diary. It's very private . . . and very personal. I won't let anyone read it.

Not even your mother? Not even your father?

Not even my mother. Not even my father.

May I look at it?

No! It's personal and private.

May I just peek at the color of the pages?

Well . . .

Please? Oh please?

All right . . . just the color of the pages.
There!

Pink! Oh, how beautiful!
May I just peek at the first word on the first page?

No!

Please? Oh please?

---

private   special, not for everyone to see
personal   having to do with oneself, not for everyone to see or know
peek   take a little look at

No!

Look. I'll let you wear my Indian bracelet.

You will! You really will? Well . . . all right, but just the first word on the first page. That's all!
There!

It says, "I." The first word is "I."
May I just peek at the second word? Please?

NO! It's personal and private.

I'll let you feed my cat.

You will! You promise? Well . . . all right, just the second word. And that's all. Understand?
There!

It says, "I think." "I think . . ."
May I just peek at the third word?

NO!

Please? Please? Please?

NO! NO! NO!

I'll let you wear my good-luck charm. The one my Aunt Grace sent from Atlantic City.

You will! All right . . . just the third word. AND THAT'S ALL! THAT IS ALL! UNDERSTAND!
There!

It says, "David." "I think David . . ."
Please, may I peek at the fourth word? Oh, please? Oh, please? Please?
Please? Please?

NO! NO! NO! NO! NO! NO! Once and for all . . . NO!

I'll let you dress my baby sister.

ALL RIGHT . . . just the fourth word. And that's the last! LAST! LAST! LAST!

It says, "is." "I think David is . . ." Is what?

I can't tell you.

It's not fair. "Is" is such a little word. It's hardly a word at all. It shouldn't have counted as a word.
Please may I see the fifth word? Please? Please? PLEASE?

NO!

If you won't let me see the fifth word, I won't be your friend.

You won't? You mean it?
There! There's the fifth word.

It says, "nice." "I think David is nice."

Do you really? Do you really think David is nice?

Uh–huh.

You like him? You really like him?

Uh–huh.
WHERE ARE YOU GOING?

To tell everybody.

COME BACK HERE!!!

Bernard Waber worked as an artist and graphic designer for several magazines before becoming a writer of  books for young people. His works are known for their warmth and sense of humor. He lives in New York City.

➤ **Bernard Waber (born 1924)** ◄

➤ *What Do You Think?*

1. What happened in the story?
2. How did the friend get the girl to tell her secret? Would that work with you?
3. What do you think is the lesson of this story?

➤ *Try This*

Reader's Theater

1. Work with a partner.
2. Each partner is one of the characters.
3. Read the story.

➤ *Learning About Language and Literature*

Ways to Write Dialogue

Quotation marks show when someone speaks. In "My Diary," the speakers are shown another way. Look back at the reading to find out how you know which character is speaking.

1. What tells you the actual words from the diary?
2. How do you know when each character speaks?

➤ *Writing*

Make a Diary

Keep a diary. Write down what you do each day for a week. Write down what you are thinking about.

WAYS TO WRITE DIALOGUE
"Everybody loves Saturday night," said Pudmoni. "I like Thursday best," replied Ahmed.
Pudmoni: Everybody loves Saturday night.   **Ahmed:** I like Thursday best.
Everybody loves Saturday night.   *I like Thursday best.*

➤ *Exploring Your Own Experience*

Talking in Code (AM)

A code is a way to write something to keep it secret. The following message is written using a "telephone code." Can you figure out what it says?

.8 4 3 / 6 .2 8. .2 .5 6. / 2. 6. .3 3 /-/ .8 .2 5. 5 3
7 7. / .9 3 7 3 /
2 7 .2 8. 3 / 7. 6. 5. .3 4. 3 7 7. //

Hint: Look at a telephone dial.

➤ *Background*

The Navajo are the largest group of Native Americans who live in the United States today. They live in the southwestern region of the United States and speak the Athabaskan language.

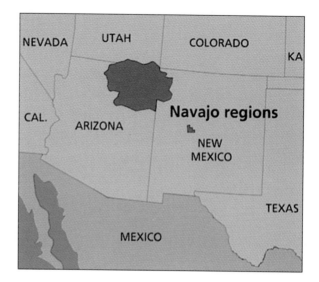

Two Navajo code talkers speaking code during the battle of Bougainville in 1943

Navajo Code Talkers

World War II. The Pacific. The U.S. was fighting Japan. The radio men were on the front lines. They sent important messages.

Messages had to be secret, of course.

They were in code. The Americans had several codes. The Japanese broke them all. Except one.

This code is Athabaskan. It is spoken by the Navajo.

There were 400 Navajo Code Talkers. All were Marines. They were trained in radio and sent to the front. There they sent messages in Athabaskan.

But it was more than that. They spoke another code in Athabaskan. It was a code inside a code. Even another Navajo could not understand it.

The code was top secret until 1968. The Navajo were ordered to tell no one. They were men of honor. They kept their secret for 20 years. So no one knew of these brave men.

Now their story is being told. In 1989, Marine General A. M. Gray spoke in Phoenix, Arizona. During the war, a lot of soldiers treated the Navajo badly. He said, "We called them 'Geronimo' and 'Chief.' It was insulting."

He had come to say, "We are sorry." And, after all this time, "Thank you."

About 250 Code Talkers are still living. About 40 heard the General speak.

Private Floyd Dann of Tuba City, Arizona, speaks in Athabaskan to other code talkers during maneuvers with the Second Army.

A Marine sergeant presents a medal to former code talker Dan Akee in 1989.

AFTER YOU READ

What Do You Think?

1. Why couldn't the Japanese break the Athabaskan code?

2. How did the Navajo Code Talkers show they were men of honor?

3. Why do you think the General came to speak to the Code Talkers?

4. *Discrimination* is when people treat someone badly because of some group the person is in. Why do you think people discriminated against the Navajo?

Try This

Sunshine Outline AM

Use a sunshine outline like the one below to summarize the story of the Navajo Code Talkers.

Who were the Navajo Code Talkers?
What did they do?
When did they use the code?
Where were they when they used the code?
Why were they needed?
How do you think the code worked?
How long did they keep the secret of the code?

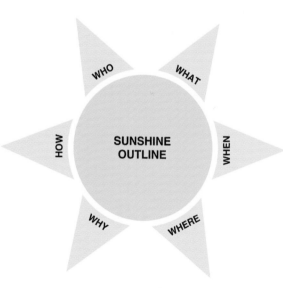

➤ Learning About Language and Literature

What Is Nonfiction?

Nonfiction is writing about things that really happened and people who really lived.

1. Look at your textbooks.
2. Which books have writing that is nonfiction?
3. Which have writing that is fiction?
4. Which have both?

LA SIGUANAVA
by Alex Aguilar

One time my uncle and some of his friends went to put the cows and the horses inside the fence. When they were finished, they had to walk about four miles down the road. When they were walking down the path, they saw La Siguanava.

The legend says that she was a princess of the Pipiles tribe. When she was a child, the Spanish conquistadors came and conquered her people. She saw how they killed her parents, the king and queen of her people. When she saw how they murdered them, she ran away. Now she has become a bad spirit.

My uncle and his friends started to run away from La Siguanava. They all made it to safety.

I believe that this story is true, because many people from my country have also seen the spirit of La Siguanava. They have told many terrible stories about her. It is better to take this story as the truth. If you ever see La Siguanava, run away as quickly as you can.

➤ Writing

Choose one of the following writing activities.

Write a Note in Code

Work with a partner. Make up a secret code of your own or use the telephone code. Write a message in your secret code. Exchange messages with your partner and decode.

Write a Nonfiction Story AM

Use a sunshine outline to outline something that really happened. Then write down the nonfiction story.

My uncle, friends, La Siguanava

They saw the bad spirit.

WHO   WHAT

Don't know

One time

HOW   SUNSHINE OUTLINE   WHEN

WHY   WHERE

El Salvador

She is sad and angry because the conquistadors killed her family and conquered her people.

➤ *Exploring Your Own Experience*

Being a Teenager AM

What do you think are the hardest things about being a teenager? What are the easiest things?

1. Work in a group of four.
2. Make a two-column chart like the one below.
3. List the hard things in one column. List the easy things in the other column.

Being a Teenager	
Easy	Hard
Having friends	School
Don't have to pay rent	Not much money

➤ *Background*

This play is based on the actual diary of a teenage Jewish girl. She wrote it while she and her family lived in hiding from the German Nazis during World War II.

The Nazis forced Jewish families and other people they didn't like to go to concentration camps. Millions of people died there.

For two years, the Franks and another Jewish family lived above an office building in Holland. They were hiding so that the Nazis wouldn't find them and send them away. Their small, secret apartment was cramped, or crowded. There was little food.

Anne wrote about the experience in her diary. She wrote about fear and joy, and about hope for a better world.

Mothers with children climb out of the freight wagon that has brought them to Auschwitz.

The Diary of Anne Frank

CHARACTERS

Narrator
Anne, a teenage girl
Margot, her older sister
Mr. Frank, Anne's father
Mrs. Frank, Anne's mother
Peter, a teenage boy
Mr. Van Daan, Peter's father
Mrs. Van Daan, Peter's mother
Mr. Kraler, building owner

SCENE 1

Narrator: The year is 1942. The Franks and the Van Daans are hiding on the second floor of Mr. Kraler's office building. It is their first night there.

Mr. Kraler: I'll come up each evening to bring you food and news. From eight in the morning until six in the evening you must be quiet. After six, my workers go home.

Mr. Frank: During the day, we will whisper when we talk. We must not run any water. The workers downstairs must not hear us. This is the way we must live until the war is over if we are to survive.

Narrator: Mr. Kraler leaves through a secret door.

Mr. Frank: After six, we can talk, laugh, and play games.

Narrator: The families start to unpack. Anne goes over to Peter. He is holding his cat.

---

survive stay alive

The film director of *The Diary of Anne Frank* views a model of the Franks' hiding place.

Anne: I love cats. I had to leave my cat behind. *(She strokes the cat.)* Where did you go to school?
Peter: Jewish Secondary.
Anne: I never saw you.
Peter: I know. But I used to see you in the yard.
Anne: Why didn't you come over?
Peter: I'm sort of a loner. *(He goes into the next room.)*
Mr. Frank *(to Anne)*: Peter is a nice boy.

Anne: He's very shy.
Mr. Frank: You'll like him.
Anne: I hope so. He's the only boy I'll be seeing for months!

SCENE 2

Narrator: Each day, Anne writes in her diary. Two months pass.
Mr. Van Daan: What's for dinner tonight?
Margot: Beans.
Mr. Van Daan: Not again!
Mr. Frank: That's all Mr. Kraler had to bring us.
Anne *(joking)*: So let's have a bean party! We have boiled beans, string beans . . .
Mr. Van Daan *(annoyed)*: Will you be quiet? Every evening you talk, talk, talk. Why aren't you quiet like Margot?
Anne: I'm different! I'm going to be a famous singer or dancer someday.
Mrs. Frank: Anne, don't answer back. Please be polite like your sister Margot.
Anne *(hurt and angry)*: Margot, Margot, Margot! Everything she does is right and everything I do is wrong! You're all against me! *(She runs out of the room crying.)*

---

loner   a person who likes to be alone

shy   afraid around people, bashful

SCENE 3

Narrator: It is December 1942. The families are celebrating the Jewish holiday *Chanukah*. They are singing holiday songs.

Anne: Now it's time for gifts!

Mrs. Frank *(sadly)*: Gifts? We have no gifts this year.

Mr. Frank: Our gift is being alive here together.

Anne *(excited)*: Wait!

Narrator: Anne leaves the room and returns with a bag of gifts. She hands her sister a crossword puzzle book.

Anne: It isn't new. It's one you've done. But I erased all your answers. You can do the whole book over again!

Margot: It's wonderful!

Anne: This is for you, Mrs. Van Daan. *(She hands her a bottle.)* It's hair shampoo. I took all the odds and ends of soap and mixed them with the last of my perfume.

Mrs. Van Daan: Oh Anne!

Anne *(to Peter)*: And this is for you.

Peter: It's a razor!

Anne: Mr. Kraler got it for me. You need a razor now. You are starting to grow a mustache.

Chanukah gift-giving scene

Dinner table scene

Narrator: Just then, they hear foot-steps downstairs.

Mr. Frank *(whispering)***:** It's probably just a thief.

Mrs. Van Daan: No! It's the police! They have found us!

Narrator: They hear the footsteps run out the door.

Mrs. Van Daan: They will come back to arrest us!

Mr. Frank: It's only a thief. He heard us and then he ran away.

Mrs. Frank: If the police catch him, he will tell them about us!

Anne *(terrified)***:** Let's get out of here!

Mr. Frank: Don't lose your faith and courage. We are still alive. It wasn't the police.

Narrator: Mr. Frank begins a prayer. One by one, the others begin to pray with him.

....

arrest stop and take to the police station
thief person who steals things

faith belief
courage bravery

SCENE 4

Narrator: A year and a half passes. Anne still writes in her diary each day. She keeps it hidden, so no one will see it. It is January 1, 1944. Peter comes to Anne's room.

Peter *(shyly)*: Anne, I want to say . . . well, if it wasn't for you, I don't know how I would last.

Anne: Thank you, Peter. This is the first time we've really talked. It helps to have someone to talk to.

Peter: Yes. I sure can't talk to my parents.

Anne: I know. The adults treat us like young children. But I think seriously about life. I want to be a writer. What do you want to do?

Peter: I think I'd like to work on a farm. I'm not very smart.

Anne: That isn't true!

Narrator: Suddenly, Anne becomes shy.

Anne: Peter, have you ever kissed a girl?

Peter: Yes. Once.

Anne: Was she pretty?

Peter: I don't know. I was blindfolded. It was a kissing game at a party.

Anne *(relieved)*: I guess that doesn't count.

Peter: No, it doesn't. *(Nervously)* I . . . I think I'd better go. It's late.

Narrator: Suddenly, Peter kisses Anne on the cheek. Then he rushes out of the room. Anne is surprised and happy.

SCENE 5

Narrator: It's late at night. Everyone is asleep. Mr. Van Daan sneaks over to the refrigerator. He takes out some bread. Mrs. Frank wakes up and sees him.

Mrs. Frank *(screaming)*: He's stealing the bread!

Margot *(waking up)*: Mr. Van Daan, that's not fair!

Mr. Van Daan: But I'm hungry!

Mrs. Van Daan: He needs more food than the rest of us. He's a big man.

Narrator: Just then, the doorbell rings.

Mr. Frank: It's Mr. Kraler! That's his signal. *(He opens the door for Mr. Kraler.)*

Mr. Kraler: I have good news! The war will soon be over!

Peter: How do you know?

Mr. Kraler: I heard it on the radio. The Germans are losing!

Narrator: Peter starts to dance around the room. Anne and Margot follow him. The adults hug each other.

Mr. Van Daan: I'm so ashamed of myself! I was stealing bread from children!

Mrs. Frank: We've all done things to be ashamed of.

Mr. Frank: Don't feel bad. The war is almost over!

Anne and Peter share a kiss.

SCENE 6

Narrator: It is an afternoon a few weeks later. The war is not over yet. Anne enters Peter's room. She tries to smile. They are both sad.

Anne *(looking out the window)*: What a lovely day. When I get tired of hiding here, I *think* myself out. I pretend I'm in the park.

Peter *(impatiently)*: When I begin to think, I get mad! We've been hiding for two years! The Nazis might still come and kill us!

Anne *(gently lifting his face)*: I think the world is still growing up. I believe that people are really good at heart. These evil things will pass. Someday, the world will be different.

Peter: I want to see something good now—not someday.

Anne *(holding his hand)*: Let's not argue like the grown-ups! Look at the sky. Isn't it lovely? Someday, when we're outside again—

Narrator: Suddenly, the doorbell starts ringing. The door downstairs crashes open.

SCENE 7

Narrator: Everyone is quiet. They hear the sound of boots coming up the stairs.

Mrs. Van Daan: Oh, no!

Peter *(hugging Anne)***:** Goodbye, Anne. *(He kisses her.)*

Narrator: The Nazi police break into the hiding place. They arrest the families. While the adults pack their belongings, Anne writes in her diary.

Anne's Diary: Dear Diary: They are waiting for us now. We can each take one bag of clothing. So, dear Diary, that means I must leave you behind. Goodbye for a little while. P.S. Please, please, Mr. Kraler, or anyone else. If you find this diary, please keep it safe for me, because someday I hope . . .

Narrator: Anne Frank died in a Nazi concentration camp. Her mother and Margot, Peter, and the Van Daans died too. Only Mr. Frank survived the camps. After the war, Mr. Frank found Anne's diary. He had it made into a book. He wanted to share Anne's dreams and hopes with the rest of the world. In this way, Anne still lives on.

----

concentration camp   prison where people were taken by the Nazis

ABOUT THE AUTHOR

Anne Frank and her family moved from Germany to the Netherlands to escape the Nazi persecution of the Jews during World War II. The Franks later were forced into hiding when the Nazis occupied the Netherlands, and during this time Anne wrote her famous diary. Soldiers discovered and captured the family, and Anne died in a concentration camp.

➤ **Anne Frank (1929–1945)** ◄

➤ *What Do You Think?*

1. Where does this play take place? Describe the place.
2. Choose an interesting character from the play. Describe that character.
3. Main events are important things that happen in a play. What are the main events of the play? Can you find a main event in each scene?
4. How is Anne Frank's life like the lives of teenagers you know? How is it different?

➤ *Try This*

Character Chairs AM

1. Label two chairs with the names of two characters in the play.
2. In groups of four, make a list of questions to ask the characters.
3. Two people sit in the chairs and try to answer questions as the characters.

Interview Questions for Peter:

| What do you think of Anne? |
| Why are you so quiet all the time? |
| Where do you want to go when you get out of the attic? |
| What do you think about . . . ? |
| How did you know . . . ? |
| When did you . . . ? |
| What would you do if . . . ? |

➤ Learning About Language and Literature

Characters, Setting, and Plot (AM)

- *Characters* are the people in a play.
- The *setting* is the time and place when the play happens.
- The *plot* is what happens.

Make a chart of the scenes of *Anne Frank* showing the characters, setting, and plot of each scene.

➤ Writing

Roundtable Scene Writing (AM)

1. Work in a group of two to four.
2. Choose a character.
3. Discuss and decide where your scene will be (the setting).
4. Discuss and decide what will happen (the plot).
5. Use one sheet of paper. Pass it from person to person.
6. Each person writes one line, taking the part of his or her character.
7. Pass the paper until the scene is done.

Characters, Setting, and Plot of a Play

Scene	Characters	Setting	Plot
1	Mr. Kraler Mr. Frank Anne Peter Narrator	The second floor of Mr. Kraler's office building, 1942	The Franks hide in the attic of the office building.
2			

➤ Making Connections

Unit Project Ideas

Here are some possible unit projects. In this project, use things you learned in the unit. You may choose to think up a project of your own and check it out with your teacher.

1. Ranking Ladder. **AM** Rank the selections in this unit. Look at the table of contents. Reread the selections. Put the one you liked best at the top of the ladder. Put the one you liked second best on the next rung, and so on. Write one sentence about each selection that tells why you ranked it the way you did.

Ranking Ladder

2. Compare and Contrast Messages. **AM** "Messages" is the theme of this unit. Choose two messages from the unit that are very different from one another. Use a Venn diagram to compare and contrast the two selections. How are they the same? How are they different? Write a paragraph describing your Venn diagram.

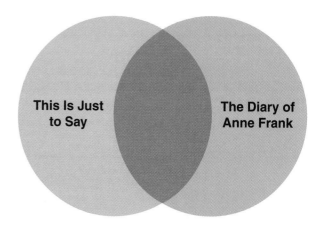

3. Signs to Music. Pick a favorite song or rap. Tape and/or perform your new rap for the class.

4. Bumper Stickers and Vanity Plates. Visit a parking lot or watch traffic for a while at a light to collect interesting bumper stickers and vanity plates (car license tags that spell out a message). Write what you think the owner means by the tag or sticker.

5. Message Magazine. Select some of the best messages, poetry, diary selections, and nonfiction writings that your class has created during the unit. Use a publishing program on a computer to make them into a magazine.

6. Reader's Theater. Rehearse and record or perform a performance or Reader's Theater production of *Anne Frank*.

7. Messages. Make a sender/receiver/mode/purpose chart for the selections in the unit. Write about how messages change for different audiences.

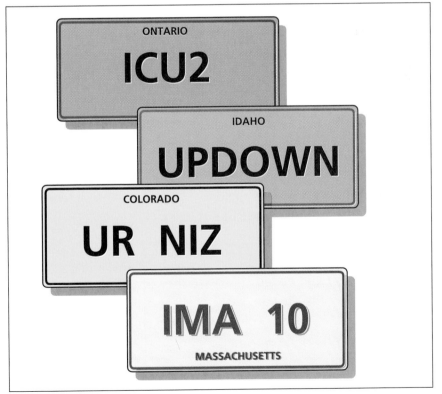

Further Reading

Following are some materials related to this unit that you might enjoy.

• ***Anne Frank: The Diary of a Young Girl.*** New York: Random House, 1947. This is a translation of the diary Anne kept during World War II while she and her family were in hiding from the Nazis.

• ***Anne Frank: Beyond the Diary: A Photographic Remembrance,*** by Rian van der Verhoeven. New York: Viking, 1993. Narration with quotations from Anne's diary accompanies photographs of her childhood, her years in hiding, and her life and death in a concentration camp.

• ***Code Busters!,*** by Burton Albert Jr. Niles, IL: Albert Whitman and Company, 1985. This book has code messages to solve that are written in dots and boxes, phone numbers, musical flags, and card decks.

• ***Codes, Ciphers, and Other Secrets,*** by Karin N. Mango. New York: Franklin Watts, 1988. This book discusses secret languages and secret writing and includes codes from the past and the present.

• ***The Collected Poems of William Carlos Williams, Volume I: 1909–1939,*** edited by A. Walton Litz and Christopher MacGowan. New York: New Directions, 1986. This volume includes almost 100 poems from the early part of Williams's career.

• ***Communication,*** by Aliki. New York: Greenwillow, 1993. This book aims to help readers learn to express their feelings and to value what others say.

• ***A Gathering of Days: A New England Girl's Journal, 1830–1832,*** by Joan W. Blos. New York: Scribner's, 1979. This is a fictional journal of a girl growing up in Maine in the 1830s. The girl reflects on an encounter with a runaway slave, the death of a friend, and her father's remarriage.

• ***Letters from Rifka,*** by Karen Hesse. New York: Holt, 1992. In letters to her cousin in Russia, 12-year-old Rifka tells of her dangerous escape across the Russian border, her trip by sea to America, and her fears while being held in detention on Ellis Island.

• ***Kinaalda: A Navajo Girl Grows Up,*** by Monty Roessel. Philadelphia: Lerner Publications, 1993. Photographs and narrative tell the story of a Navajo girl who participates in the traditional coming-of-age ceremony of her people.

• ***The Navajos,*** by Peter Iverson. New York: Chelsea House, 1990. This book gives a history of the Navajo people from the 1800s, when they first met white settlers, up to the present. It also includes pictures of Navajo silver and wool crafts.

- **"Navajo Code Talkers: A Few Good Men,"** by Bruce Watson. In *Smithsonian,* 24:5, pp. 34–45, August 1993. This article explains how the Code Talkers helped the Allied forces win World War II.

- **'Til All the Stars Have Fallen,** selections by David Booth. New York: Viking Penguin, 1989. David Booth, an education professor from Toronto, has collected (mostly) Canadian poems from many cultures, including some concrete or "shape" poems.

- **Voices and Visions: William Carlos Williams.** New York Center for Visual History, 1988. This video is a collage of historical footage, interviews, animation, and dramatization of the poet's work.

- **Maus: A Survivor's Tale,** by Art Spiegelman. New York: Pantheon Books, 1986. Maus II: And Here My Troubles Began. Art Spiegelman. New York: Pantheon Books, 1991. Art Spiegelman tells a serious story in cartoon format in these two books about his father's life before, during and after the Holocaust. These books deal with the emotional effects of the Holocaust on the survivor and his family, including his son. Spiegelman won a Pulitzer Prize for these works.

Multicultural Group of People by Tony Ortega, 1992

People

People come in many shapes and colors. This unit shows some of the ways that people are different from one another. The main focus, however, is on how we are the same. People around the world face similar challenges and conflicts.

➤ *Exploring Your Own Experience*

Moving AM

1. Work in small groups.
2. Discuss a time when you moved from one place to another.
3. Use a map to show the group where you lived before and after your move.

Venn Diagram: Then and Now AM

A Venn diagram helps you compare two things. Make a Venn diagram like the one below to help you compare your life before and after your move.

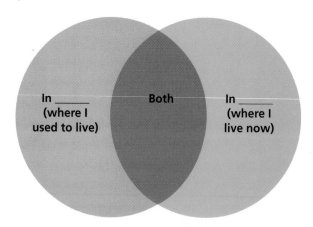

In _____
(where I
used to live)

Both

In _____
(where I
live now)

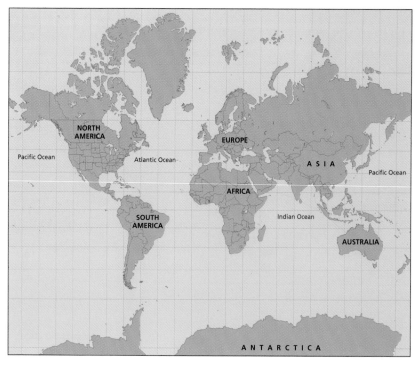

➤ *Background*

The following poem is about the life of a boy who left El Salvador for North America. Trace his travels on the map.

Below are some of the fruits Miguel ate in El Salvador.

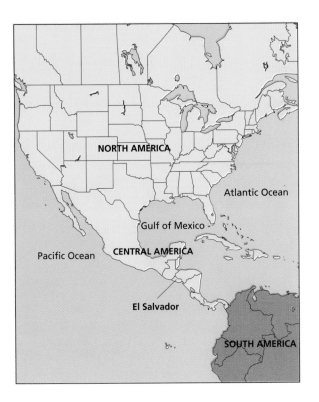

We Ask for Peace by Pablo Mayorga, circa 1983

Miguel en el Norte

by Jorge Argueta

In El Salvador
Miguel's life
was one of
mangos, guayabas, and nizperos,
starry nights,
rivers filled with nests,
and green meadows
to run through with joy.

But one day Miguel
was forced to leave
his country.
He fled to the North,
where everything is cold and foggy,
and they speak English.

mangos, guayabas, nizperos tropical fruits
meadows grassland
forced made to do something without choice
fled ran away
foggy misty, with clouds low to the ground

But Miguel doesn't speak
any English.
He can say
hi, yes, bye, and no,
but that's about it.

Miguel is sad.
He yearns for
the mango trees,
the guayabas,
the nizperos,
and the green meadows
to run through with joy.

....

yearns   wants, longs for

Jorge Argueta is a poet from El Salvador who has published three books since he came to the United States. He wrote "Miguel en el Norte" to describe the experience of his young nephews who left El Salvador because of the civil war there, and who miss their country very much.

➤ **Jorge Argueta (born 1961)** ◄

AFTER YOU READ

➤ What Do You Think?

1. How do you picture Miguel? How old is he? What does he look like?
2. What was Miguel's life like in El Salvador?
3. How does he feel now? Why?
4. How do you think he will feel in two years?

➤ Learning About Language and Literature

Mood/Tone AM

The overall feeling of a literary work is called the *mood* or *tone*. A poem's mood might be happy or angry or sad or afraid. What mood do you think the author of this poem expresses? What words or phrases convey that mood?

1. Study the chart below. Notice that colors are used to show moods.
2. Find words or phrases in the poem "Miguel en el Norte" that express the moods at the top of the column.
3. Write the words in the boxes underneath the "mood" word. Write them in the "mood" color shown in the key.

Words Show Moods

Happy	Angry	Sad	Afraid
green meadows	forced	cold, foggy	doesn't speak any English

Key:

- yellow: happy
- red: angry
- blue: sad
- orange: afraid

➤ Try This

Moods in Color AM

1. Copy "Miguel en el Norte" using colored pencils or markers.
2. Write each part of the poem with the color the words make you think of or feel.
3. Make a key for colors you choose. Tell what mood each color shows.
4. Tell a partner why you used the colors you did.
5. Discuss with the class the mood of this poem.

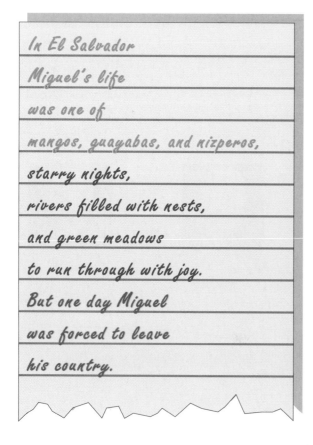

In El Salvador
Miguel's life
was one of
mangos, guayabas, and nizperos,
starry nights,
rivers filled with nests,
and green meadows
to run through with joy.
But one day Miguel
was forced to leave
his country.

➤ Writing

Choose a writing activity:

A Letter AM

1. Write a letter to Miguel.
2. Tell him that you are sorry for his troubles.
3. Give him some advice to help him feel more comfortable in the North.

A Poem AM

1. Use the ideas from the Venn diagram you made to write a poem about a time when you moved.
2. Use a thesaurus or translation dictionary to find words that show the mood or tone of your poem.
3. Write the poem with colored markers or pencils that show your mood.
4. Share your draft with a classmate. Revise, edit, and share with the whole class.

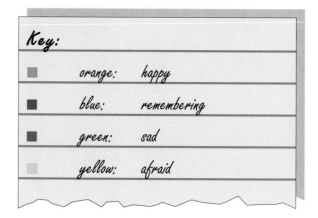

Key:
- orange: happy
- blue: remembering
- green: sad
- yellow: afraid

➤ Exploring Your Own Experience AM

1. What do families like to do together? Share ideas.
2. Draw a picture of your family doing something together.
3. Label all the people and things in the picture.
4. Tell a partner about your picture.

➤ Background

A woman who lives in the state of Georgia, in the south of the United States, painted the picture on page 132 and wrote the story. She was born on March 30, 1908. She tells about her life in the hills of north Georgia when she was a little girl. Before you read Mattie Lou O'Kelley's story, study her painting.

1. What is the painting about?
2. How would you describe the style of the painting?
3. How many objects and activities in the painting can you name?

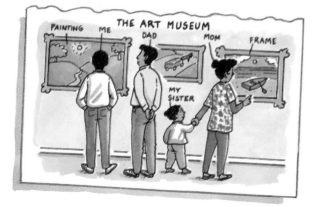

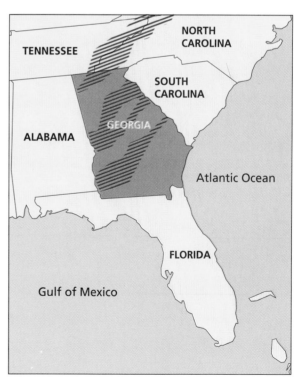

Family Gathering by Mattie Lou O'Kelley, 1982

Family Gathering

by Mattie Lou O'Kelley

Our house is jammed full on the Sundays when the whole family comes for the day.

Mama cooks up a storm for our midday dinner, and if we're lucky, Papa grates some sweet potatoes for Mama's special sweet potato pudding.

There's not much doll playing in our family, so after dinner all of us kids go outside to pitch horseshoes and play leapfrog and shoot marbles. Sometimes we catch june bugs and tie string to their legs.

When it's evening, the aunts and uncles pile sleepy cousins into their wagons and make their way home.

---

jammed   packed, filled

cooks up a storm   cooks a lot of food

grates   uses a kitchen tool to shred into small pieces

pudding   a soft, sweet food made with eggs and milk

pitch horseshoes   play a game throwing horseshoes so that they land around a metal stake

leapfrog   a game in which children crouch down while others jump over them

marbles   a game with small colored glass balls

june bugs   large beetles

Mattie Lou O'Kelley was almost 60 years old when she began her painting career. Her colorful folk art has been displayed in museums and in children's books. She portrays images from her childhood memories of rural Georgia.

➤ **Mattie Lou O'Kelley (born 1908)** ◄

➤ *Background* (AM)

The following painting and story are by a Mexican-American woman who grew up in a small town in Texas. She paints and writes about her life in Texas as a little girl. Before you read Carmen Lomas Garza's story, study her painting. Use a Venn diagram to compare and contrast the two paintings.

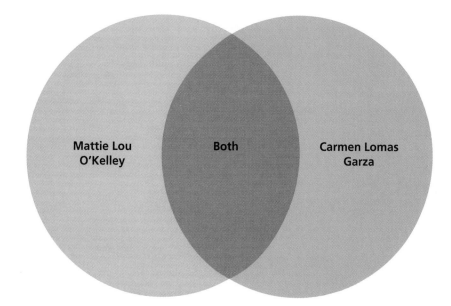

Mattie Lou O'Kelley   **Both**   **Carmen Lomas Garza**

Making Tamales by Carmen Lomas Garza, 1987

Making Tamales

by Carmen Lomas Garza

This is a scene from my parents' kitchen. Everybody is making tamales. My grandfather is wearing blue overalls and a blue shirt. I'm right next to him with my sister Margie. We're helping to soak the dried leaves from the corn. My mother is spreading the cornmeal dough on the leaves and my aunt and uncle are spreading meat on the dough. My grandmother is lining up the rolled and folded tamales ready for cooking. In some families just the women make tamales, but in our family everybody helps.

---

soak   cover with water and leave for a while

dough   an uncooked mixture of flour, liquid, and other ingredients for baking

Carmen Lomas Garza is a Mexican American artist who lives in San Francisco. *Family Pictures/ Cuadros de Familia* is a  bilingual picture book of Garza's paintings about her family life growing up in a Hispanic community in southern Texas.

➤ **Carmen Lomas Garza** ◄

➤ What Do You Think?

1. What are Mattie Lou O'Kelley's family members doing?

2. What are Carmen Lomas Garza's family members doing?

3. Does the picture match the story in each of these? Which tells more, the painting or the story?

➤ Try This

Who Is Doing What? AM

Use the chart below to describe what is happening in these two captioned pictures.

Who Is Doing What?				
Who?	What is the person doing?	Did you find out from the text or the picture or both?	Is this person in the O'Kelley or the Garza captioned picture?	Would you like to do this? Why or why not?
Man in moustache	soaking corn husks	both	Garza	Yes. I'd like to do it so I could eat the tamales.

➤ *Learning About Language and Literature*

A Caption

A caption is the writing that tells what is happening in a picture.

1. Bring a photo of your family, or select a family photo from a magazine.
2. Write a caption for the photo. Use either the present tense or the past tense in your caption.
3. Exchange captions and photos with a partner. Check to see that your partner's caption is all written in the same tense.

Mom, Dad, my brother, and I are bicycling.

➤ *Writing*

Description AM

Writers make their writing interesting and colorful by describing things. They write so that you can picture in your mind what they write about. They choose interesting facts to share with the reader.

1. Use your family photograph from the last activity, or select one from a book or magazine.
2. Label all the people and things in the picture. Look up the words you don't know. Use a picture dictionary or translation dictionary.
3. Label the feelings the people in the picture are experiencing.
4. Write about your picture. Use the words from your label and caption.
5. Read your writing and/or tell the class about your picture. Include some interesting facts in your description.
6. Revise your writing and put it on the page with your picture.

➤ Exploring Your Own Experience

Brave People Hunt (AM)

1. Think about someone brave. What are three words that describe this person? What brave thing did the person do? Write the answers on a chart like the one below.

2. Ask your classmates about the brave person they know. Write their answers on your chart.

3. Make a class list of brave people and words that describe them.

➤ Background

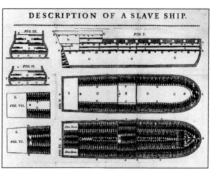

DESCRIPTION OF A SLAVE SHIP.

Published in 1789, the "Description of a Slave Ship" showed seven views of the ships, which were made to get the greatest number of captives on board.

The Underground Railroad, done after a painting by Webber (undated), shows a group of slaves being freed after a long and tiresome journey.

		Brave People Hunt		
Name of class member	Name of brave person	How you know about the person	Three terms that describe the person	Something brave the person did and why
Mia	Martin Luther King, Jr.	TV, my mom, books	good speaker nonviolent minister	led a bus strike so people could sit where they wanted

Harriet Tubman **141**

Harriet Tubman Series No. 10 by Jacob Lawrence, 1939–40

Harriet Tubman

by Eloise Greenfield

Harriet Tubman didn't take no stuff
Wasn't scared of nothing neither
Didn't come in this world to be no slave
And wasn't going to stay one either

"Farewell!" she sang to her friends one night
She was mighty sad to leave 'em
But she ran away that dark, hot night
Ran looking for her freedom

She ran to the woods and she ran through the
 woods
With the slave catchers right behind her
And she kept on going till she got to the North
Where those mean men couldn't find her

---

didn't take no stuff   didn't let people tell her what to do or
let them say bad things to her
scared   afraid
'em   them (dialect)
slave catchers   people who were paid money to catch
runaway slaves and return them to their owners
till   until

Nineteen times she went back South
To get three hundred others
She ran for her freedom nineteen times
To save Black sisters and brothers
Harriet Tubman didn't take no stuff
Wasn't scared of nothing neither
Didn't come in this world to be no slave
And didn't stay one either

And didn't stay one either.

ABOUT THE AUTHOR

Eloise Greenfield has written picture books, poetry, novels, and biographies of African American heroes. Her writings for children stress positive attitudes and the importance of the family.

➤ **Eloise Greenfield (born 1929)** ◄

AFTER YOU READ

➤ *What Do You Think?*

1. Why did Harriet Tubman run away?
2. Why did she go back nineteen times?
3. Why did she run in the woods at night?
4. Was Harriet brave? Why or why not?

➤ *Try This*

Point of View

Group Work

1. Work in four groups. Use a chart like the one below. (You might also choose to include characters like the narrator or the people who helped Harriet and her "Black sisters and brothers" along the way.)
2. In each box, write questions you would like to ask.

Class Activity

1. Four students stand in front of the class. Each person plays the part of the point of view of a different character.
2. Class members ask them the questions on their charts.
3. The point of view characters answer the questions from their points of view.

Point of View	
Harriet Tubman	**Slave Owner**
1. Why did you run away?	1. How do you feel about owning another human being?
2. Why did you go back?	2.
Tree in the Forest	**Slave Catcher**
1. How did you help Harriet and her friends?	1. Why were you a slave catcher?
2.	2.

Learning About Language and Literature

Narrative Poetry AM

Sometimes poetry tells a story. In the poem "Harriet Tubman," Eloise Greenfield tells the true story of a woman who ran away from slavery and then returned to help others run away.

Use the story sequence outline below to outline the parts of the story of Harriet Tubman.

Writing

Narrative Poem or Prose AM

1. Use the chart on page 141 to outline your own story.
2. Write about the brave person you thought of in the "Brave People Hunt" activity. Use your notes on the chart on page 141.
3. Using your outline, tell a partner about your story.
4. Ask your partner questions about his or her story.
5. Revise your story. Illustrate it, if you like.

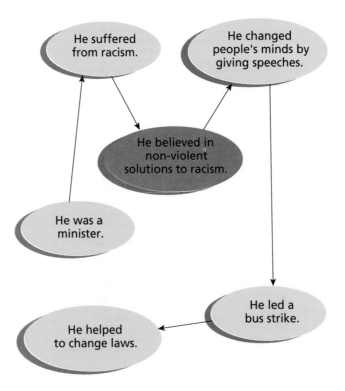

➤ Exploring Your Own Experience

Playing a Trick AM

Do you know of a story (real or not) in which people get what they want by playing a trick?

1. Make a story map of your story.

2. Fill in the circles with pictures and/or words.

3. Use your map to share your story with classmates.

What Is a Usurer?

The following story comes from Vietnam. One character in the story is a rich man who is a usurer. A usurer is someone who lends people money and charges a lot of money in interest. Today we sometimes call people like this "loan sharks." In the southwestern United States they call them "coyotes."

➤ Background

Where Is Vietnam?

Find Vietnam and its neighbors on the map.

Stage Directions

The following story is told as a play. Take different parts as you read. Do not read the words in parentheses [( )]. These are stage directions, which tell you how to read or what to do. Practice reading showing different emotions.

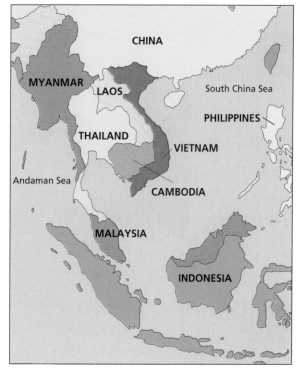

Southeast Asia

A farm village in Vietnam, long ago

The Fly

**A Reader's Theater Script,
Adapted from Jane Yolen's Version**

CHARACTERS:

Narrator
Rich Man, the moneylender
Child
Peasant Husband
Peasant Wife
Mandarin, governor of the county

SETTING:

A farm village in Vietnam, long ago

Narrator: Everyone in the village knew the moneylender, a rich and smart man. Although he owned a fortune, he was still not happy with what he had, so the man went on making money by lending it to people all over the county at exorbitant rates. Numerous people in the area owed money to the usurer.

One day, the rich man set out for the house of one of the peasant families to collect money. These peasants just could not manage to pay off his longstanding debt. Working themselves to shadows, the peasants barely succeeded in making ends meet. The money-

---

fortune   a lot of money—more than enough money to live on for the rest of your life

exorbitant   unfairly high

longstanding   lasting for a long time

---

debt   money owed

working themselves to shadows   working so long and hard that they became very thin

making ends meet   having just enough money to live

Numerous people in the area owed money to the usurer.

Narrator: But the little child went on playing and did not answer.

Rich Man *(angry)*: Child, where are your parents?

Child: Well, sir, my father has gone to cut living trees and plant dead ones and my mother is at the marketplace selling the wind and buying the moon.

Rich Man: What? What in heaven are you talking about? Quick, tell me where they are, or you will see what this stick can do to you!

Narrator: The big, rich man shook the bamboo walking stick in his hand.

Child: Sir, it's true. My father has gone to cut living trees and plant dead ones and my mother is at the marketplace selling the wind and buying the moon.

Rich Man *(exasperated)*: All right, little devil, listen to me! I came here today to take the money your parents owe me. But if you tell me where they really are and what they are doing, I will forget all about the debt. Is that clear to you?

Narrator: For the first time the child looked interested.

Child: Oh, sir, why are you joking with a poor little child? Do you expect me to believe what you are saying?

Rich Man: Well, there is heaven and there is earth to witness my promise. *(He points up to the sky and down to the ground.)*

lender decided that if he could not get his money back this time, he would take some of his debtors' most valuable belongings. But the rich man found no one at the peasants' house but a small child of eight or nine playing alone in the dirt yard.

Rich Man: Child, are your parents home?

Child: No, sir.

Narrator: The child went on playing with sticks and stones, paying no attention whatever to the man.

Rich Man *(in an irritated voice)*: Then, where are they?

"Sir, it's true. My father has gone to cut living trees and plant dead ones and my mother is at the marketplace selling the wind and buying the moon."

Child (*laughing*): Sir, heaven and earth cannot talk and therefore cannot testify. I want some living thing to be our witness.

Narrator: The Rich Man caught sight of a fly alighting on a bamboo pole nearby. He laughed to himself because he was fooling the child.

Rich Man: There is a fly. It can be our witness. Now, hurry and tell me what you mean when you say that your father is out cutting living trees and planting dead ones, while your mother is at the market selling the wind and buying the moon.

Child (*looking at the fly on the pole*): A fly is a good enough witness for me. Well, here it is, sir. My father has simply gone to cut down bamboos and make a fence with them for a man near the river. And my mother . . . oh, sir, you'll keep your promise, won't you? You will free my parents of all their debts? You really mean it?

Rich Man: Yes, yes, I do solemnly swear in front of this fly here.

Child: Well, my mother, she has gone to the market to sell fans so she can buy oil for our lamps. Isn't that what you would call selling the wind to buy the moon?

Rich Man (*shaking his head*): I guess so. Farewell. I will soon return to make good my promise.

Narrator: A few days had passed when the moneylender returned. This time he found the poor peasant couple at home, for it was late in the evening. A nasty scene ensued.

Rich Man (*angry*): Now it's time for you to pay the money you owe me.

testify   swear to tell the truth in court and do so

witness   a person who testifies in court about something he or she saw

alighting   setting down
solemnly   very seriously
nasty   bad, unpleasant
ensued   happened next

Peasant Wife: I'm sorry, we've worked ourselves to the bone, but we don't have the money yet. Please give us just a little more time!

Rich Man *(exasperated)*: I've given you time over and over again. Pay me the money or let me take your things. And do it now!

Peasant Husband: Oh, please, take pity on us, sir. Just a little more time!

Narrator: Their argument awakened the little child, who ran to the parents.

Child: Father, Mother, you don't have to pay your debt. This gentleman here has promised me that he would forget all about the money you owe him.

Rich Man *(shaking his stick at the whole family)*: Nonsense! Are you going to stand there and listen to a child's inventions? I never spoke a word to this child. Now, tell me, are you going to pay or are you not?

Narrator: Since the rich man and the peasants could not agree, they brought their problem before the mandarin who governed the county. Not knowing what to believe, all the poor peasants could do was to bring their child with them when they went to court. The little child's insistence about the rich

Since the rich man and the peasants could not agree, they brought their problem before the mandarin who governed the county.

man's promise was their only encouragement.

Mandarin: Tell me exactly what happened between you and this moneylender.

Narrator: Happily, the child hastened to tell about the explanations she gave the rich man in exchange for the debt.

Child: And he solemnly swore that he

---

inventions made-up or imaginary ideas
mandarin governor of the county
insistence taking a stand and not giving it up

encouragement reason to continue
hastened hurried

would forgive all my parents' debt if I told him what they were doing. So I did.

Mandarin: Well, if this man here has indeed made such a promise, we have only your word for it. How do we know that you have not invented the whole story yourself? In a case like this, you need a witness to confirm it, and you have none.

Child *(calmly)*: But, naturally, there was a witness.

Mandarin: Who is that, child?

Child: A fly, Your Honor.

Mandarin *(becoming stern)*: A fly? What do you mean, a fly? Watch out, child, fantasies are not to be tolerated in this place!

Child: Yes, Your Honor, a fly. *(leaping up)* A fly which was alighting on this gentleman's nose!

Rich Man *(roaring angrily and red-faced)*: Insolent little devil, that's a pack of lies! The fly was *not* on my nose; *it was on the housepole. . . .*

Narrator: The usurer stopped dead. It was, however, too late. Everyone, even the rich man, slowly started to laugh.

Mandarin *(laughing)*: Now, now, that's all settled. You have indeed made your promises, dear sir, to the child. *Housepole or no housepole, your conversation did happen after all!* The court says you must keep your promise. *(still chuckling)* Now you are all dismissed.

....

chuckling   laughing a little

"A fly is a good enough witness for me."

➤ *What Do You Think?*

1. What did the usurer want? What did the family want? Could everyone have what they wanted?

2. How did the child trick the usurer into forgiving the debt? Do you think the child did this on purpose?

3. How did the child prove to the mandarin what happened?

4. Were you happy with the ending? Why or why not?

➤ *Try This*

Open Mind Diagram

1. Work in small groups.

2. Each group chooses one of these characters: the usurer, the child, the mandarin.

3. Make an "Open Mind" diagram to describe your character. Use a dictionary, translation dictionary, or thesaurus to help you.

4. Share your diagram with the class.

I just can't get enough money. Maybe I can get some more from these poor people.

➤ Learning About Language and Literature

Surprises in Literature

One of the things that makes a selection interesting to the reader is surprise. The author leads the reader to expect one thing, and then something surprising or unexpected happens.

1. Can you find a surprise in this play?

2. Look back over other selections in this book. Can you find things that you didn't expect?

3. Does finding something unexpected make the literature more interesting to you? Why or why not?

➤ Writing

Write a Dialogue AM

In a play, a dialogue is a conversation between two people.

1. Work in pairs to write a dialogue that tells a story.

2. Each person needs a different color piece of paper.

3. Each person takes the part of one person in the dialogue and writes the lines, or words, of that person on his or her paper.

4. Take turns writing lines, and help your partner when it is his or her turn. Try to make something in your dialogue surprising.

5. Cut your colored paper into strips. Glue the lines on a third piece of paper in order.

6. Read your dialogue to the class.

Excuse me, where is your mother?

My mother is busy hunting between heaven and earth.

Where is your father?

My father is busy making many out of few.

That doesn't make any sense!

Yes, it does!

I'll give you a dollar if you tell me what they're really doing.

I already did. My mother is picking cherries in the tree. My father is planting beans in the garden.

I give up! Here's your dollar

Unit Follow-Up

➤ Making Connections

Unit Project Ideas

Here are some possible unit projects. You may also choose to think up a project of your own. Be sure to tell your teacher. Use some of the strategies and concepts you learned in the unit to plan and complete your project.

1. People Songs.

- Find a song or songs that describe a character.
- Write down the words to the song.
- Tell the class what you learned about the character. You can use an "Open Mind Diagram" to show what the character is thinking.

2. Storyboard. **AM** Make a storyboard about the life of a famous person you admire.

- Read about the person, or watch a video.
- Make a storyboard about important events in that person's life.
- Write a caption in each box. Include the date and place of the event.
- Display your storyboard and tell your classmates about it.

3. Comic Strip. **AM** Draw and write a comic strip about a character you know or one from the readings.

- Draw a series of pictures that tell a story about the character. You can use the storyboard form on page 15.
- Try to include a surprise.
- Use "balloons" coming from characters' mouths to show what they say.
- Share your comic strip with friends and/or submit it to the school paper.

4. People Collage. Which are more important—differences between people or similarities? Make a collage of pictures of people. Write descriptions to show your answer to this question.

5. Interview and Character Sketch. A character sketch is a short description of a person that tells a story or stories so you get to know the person. Interview someone interesting and write a character sketch.

6. People Database. Make a database about people. Put your database on a chart or on a computer. Your fields might include last name, first name, country of birth, favorite food, favorite music, favorite color, quote from the person, favorite sport, favorite movie star, future plans.

Further Reading AM

Following are some materials related to this unit that you might enjoy.

• *From the Hills of Georgia,* by Mattie Lou O'Kelley. Boston: Atlantic Monthly Press, 1983. Mattie Lou O'Kelley drew from her experiences of growing up on a farm in the southern United States to create these 28 bright and colorful folk paintings.

• *Mattie Lou O'Kelley: Folk Artist.* Boston: Little, Brown, 1989. O'Kelley's paintings feature scenes of animals, people, and activities during all four seasons.

• *Harriet Tubman and the Underground Railroad.* Highstown, NY: McGraw-Hill Training Systems, 1964. This film dramatizes the 19 trips Harriet Tubman made into slave territory between 1850 and 1860.

• *Honey, I Love,* by Eloise Greenfield. New York: Crowell, 1978. Greenfield's poetry looks at life as seen by a young girl. In these 16 poems she talks about riding on a train, playing games with her friends, and sharing love with her family. This collection includes the poem "Harriet Tubman."

• *Family Pictures,* by Carmen Lomas Garza. San Francisco: Children's Book Press, 1990. A famous Mexican American painter uses words and pictures to share her childhood memories of growing up in a Hispanic community in southern Texas. The author deals with everyday experiences like picking oranges as well as special activities such as going to a Mexican fair.

• *Favorite Folktales from Around the World,* edited by Jane Yolen. New York: Pantheon Books, 1986. This book, which includes "The Fly," collects witty, wise, and scary stories from many different countries in Asia, Europe, and North America. It includes tales about heroes, fools, shape shifters, and ghosts.

• *The Land I Lost: Adventures of a Boy in Vietnam,* by Huynh Quang Nhuong. New York: Harper and Row, 1986. The author shares amazing and exciting childhood adventures of village life in Vietnam before the Vietnam War.

• *The Season of Secret Wishes,* by Iva Prochazkova. New York: Lothrop, Lee & Shepard, 1989. Kapka is an 11-year-old girl living in Czechoslovakia right before the country becomes a democracy. After Kapka's father is turned away from a government-sponsored art show, he gets in trouble with the officials for displaying his sculptures in a private street exhibition.

The Peaceable Kingdom by Edward Hicks, 1847

UNIT

5

Peace

This unit is about the hopes
people have for peace—
peace among people in their
daily lives and peace among
nations around the world.

➤ *Exploring Your Own Experience*

Peace Brainstorm AM

1. What does "peace" mean to you? Can you describe it without using the word "no"?

2. Name the places where you live and go to school using the categories on the circles chart below. Can you think of a peaceful situation in each of these places?

3. Draw or describe a peaceful situation in one of these places:
   - At home
   - At school
   - In your neighborhood
   - In your city or town
   - In your country
   - Between countries

   Use a chart like the one on the following page to help you.

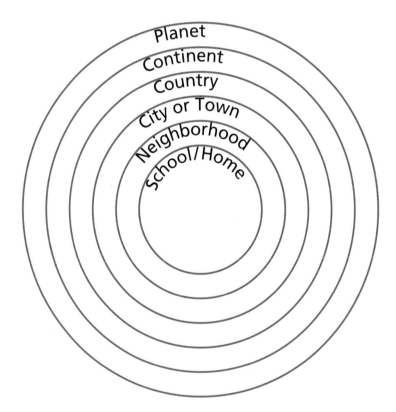

Planet
Continent
Country
City or Town
Neighborhood
School/Home

➤ Background

As the twenty-first century is about to begin, there are civil wars going on in over 100 countries. The following poem suggests what each person can do for peace.

A peaceful moment can be as simple as reading a book under a shady tree.

Peaceful Places	
Place	Peaceful Moments
Home	playing with my baby sister
	reading a book
School	
Neighborhood	
Town or City	
Country	

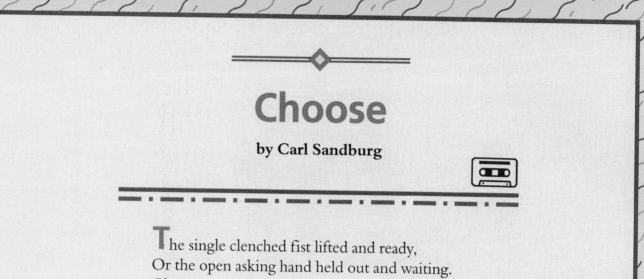

Choose

by Carl Sandburg

The single clenched fist lifted and ready,
Or the open asking hand held out and waiting.
Choose:
For we meet by one or the other.

---

clenched brought together tightly
lifted held up

Carl Sandburg, the son of a black-smith, earned his own living from the age of 13. His love of the United States is evident in his many poems and also in his Pulitzer Prize-winning, six-volume biography of Abraham Lincoln. The famous words of Lincoln himself can actually be used to describe Sandburg. He was "of the people, by the people, for the people."

➤ **Carl Sandburg (1878–1967)** ◄

AFTER YOU READ

➤ *What Do You Think?*

1. What is the choice the poet offers?
2. Have you had a choice like this?
3. What happened?
4. Do countries have the same choices as individuals?

➤ *Try This*

Finding a Win–Win Solution **AM**

1. Work with a partner.
2. Discuss one of the problems below.
3. Try to find a solution in which both people win.
4. Write your answer on chart paper or on the board.
5. Read everyone's answers and discuss.

FIND A WIN-WIN SOLUTION

A. A student is sitting in the best seat on the bus. Another student comes up and says, "You're sitting in my seat!"

B. As a joke, a student takes another student's backpack and hides it. The student whose backpack has been stolen doesn't think it's funny.

C. Two students talk about a third student behind his or her back. The third student finds out and is not happy.

➤ Learning About Language and Literature

Imagery

When writing makes you see a picture in your mind, it is called *visual imagery.* Good writers help you see very clear pictures.

1. As you read "Choose," what pictures did you see in your mind?
2. Draw a picture of what you saw.
3. Discuss your pictures with a partner.

➤ Writing

A Choice

1. Write about a choice you have had or that you might have.
2. Write so that your reader can see a picture.
3. Don't tell which choice you made: let your reader make his or her *own* choice.
4. Exchange papers with a partner. Read and discuss.

➤ Exploring Your Own Experience

Problem-Solving Wheel **AM**

This wheel shows the different ways that problems can be resolved.

1. Think of a problem that you had.
2. How did you resolve the problem?
3. Which part of the wheel shows the way you resolved the problem?

➤ Background

The Surrender Speech of Chief Joseph

Joseph was chief of the Nez Percé, a Native American tribe of Oregon. In 1877 they were ordered to a *reservation*, or special land reserved for Native Americans. The Nez Percé refused to go. Instead, Chief Joseph tried to lead 800 of his people to Canada. Fighting the U.S. Army all along the way, they crossed Idaho and Montana. They were trapped just forty miles from Canada. After a five-day fight, they were beaten.

It was then that Chief Joseph made his speech of surrender.

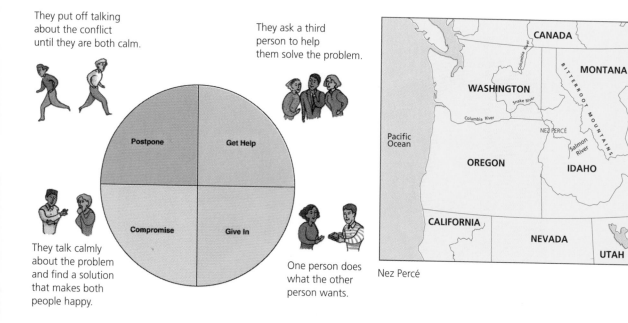

They put off talking about the conflict until they are both calm.

They ask a third person to help them solve the problem.

Postpone

Get Help

Compromise

Give In

They talk calmly about the problem and find a solution that makes both people happy.

One person does what the other person wants.

Nez Percé

Chief Joseph

I Will Fight No More Forever

Surrender Speech by Chief Joseph, Nez Percé

I am tired of fighting. Our chiefs are killed. Looking Glass is dead. Toohulhulsote is dead. The old men are all dead. It is the young men who say yes or no. He who led the young men is dead.

It is cold and we have no blankets. The little children are freezing to death. My people, some of them, have run away to the hills and have no blankets, no food. No one knows where they are—perhaps freezing to death. I want to have time to look for my children and see how many I can find. Maybe I shall find them among the dead.

Hear me, my chiefs. I am tired. My heart is sick and sad. From where the sun now stands, I will fight no more forever.

The U.S. government forced Chief Joseph and the Nez Percé tribe to settle in what is now Oklahoma. Joseph later moved to a reservation in the state of Washington.

➤ **Chief Joseph (1840?–1904)** ◄

➤ *What Do You Think?*

1. How does this selection make you feel? Why?

2. Why do you think Chief Joseph made the decision he did?

3. What do you think the young men thought about Chief Joseph's decision? The old men? The women? The children? The soldiers?

4. Do you think Chief Joseph made the right decision? Why or why not?

➤ *Learning About Language and Literature*

How Do You Write a Speech?

A speech is meant to be spoken. It usually tries to change people's minds about something. Here are some characteristics of good speeches:

- Sentences are short and clear.
- Structure is simple and clear.
- Words are strong and memorable.

Can you think of anything else that helps make a good speech?

Characteristics of a Good Speech	
Name of Speaker:	
Characteristic	*Examples in the Speech*
Short, clear sentences	
Simple, clear structure	
Strong, memorable words	

➤ *Try This* (AM)

1. Look back at the speech of Chief Joseph.

2. Can you find the characteristics of a good speech in this one?

3. Use the chart on page 171 to help you. List examples from Chief Joseph's speech.

➤ *Writing*

Write a Letter (AM)

1. Think of something you want to happen or change.

For example, you might want:

- a ride home from school
- a way to fix a mistake on your test
- to turn a vacant lot near your house into a park
- to make your school safer

2. Think of someone who can make it happen.

3. Think of three or four reasons why the person should help make it happen.

4. Write the reasons in a letter.

5. Following is an outline of the format for a letter. Use it to help you.

(Date)

(Address of person)

(City, state or province, zip code)

Dear_____,

   I am writing this letter to ask you to _____ .

   I think you should do this because _____ .

   Thank you for your time.

Sincerely,

_____

(Your name)

➤ *Exploring Your Own Experience*

Quickwrite

Did anyone ever speak up for you when you needed help? Think about it.

1. Start to write about that time.

2. Write until your teacher tells you to stop.

3. When you finish, read your Quickwrite to a partner.

4. After you have read the Quickwrites, talk about them.

➤ *Background*

Before and during World War II, the German Nazis imprisoned and killed millions of people because of their political beliefs, religion, nationality, race, sexual orientation, or disabilities. The author of the following poem lived in Europe during that time.

Fear not your enemies for they can only kill you
Fear not your friends for they can only betray you
Fear only the indifferent who permit the killers
and betrayers to walk safely on earth

E. Yashinski

Indifference by Fritz Hirschberger, 1990

On Speaking Up for Each Other

by Martin Niemöller

In Germany they came first for the Communists,
and I didn't speak up
because I wasn't a Communist.

Then they came for the Jews,
And I didn't speak up
because I wasn't a Jew.

Then they came for the trade
unionists, and I didn't speak up
because I wasn't a trade unionist.

Communists   members of the Communist political group
Jews   followers of the Jewish religion
trade unionists   workers who form a group to help improve pay and
working conditions

Then they came for the Catholics,
and I didn't speak up
because I was a Protestant.

Then they came for me,
and by that time
no one was left to speak up.

....

Catholics   followers of the Catholic religion
Protestant   follower of a Christian religion that is not Catholic

ABOUT THE AUTHOR

The Reverend Martin Niemöller, a Protestant minister from Germany, was a prisoner in Nazi concentration camps during World War II. He served as president of the World Council of Churches during the 1960s.

➤ **Martin Niemöller (1892–1984)** ◄

AFTER YOU READ

➤ *What Do You Think?*

1. Why do you think the speaker of the poem didn't speak up?

2. What happened when no one spoke up?

3. What words or phrases are repeated in the poem? What effect does that have?

➤ *Try This*

Fishbone

1. Work in a small group.

2. Draw a fishbone picture like the one below.

3. Write what happened in the poem on the fishbones.

4. Write the result on the fish head.

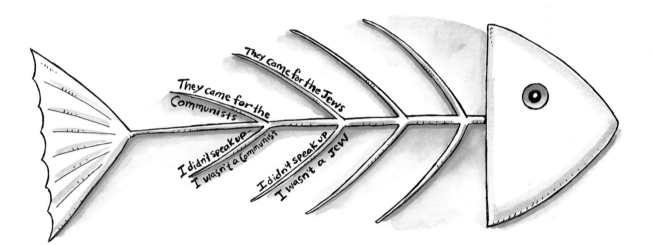

➤ Learning About Language and Literature

Structure AM

The writer of this poem used a structure, or plan, so that the writing would make sense. This structure helps hold the poem together and be powerful just as bone structure holds a fish together.

1. Copy the poem.
2. Write down the first line of each stanza.
3. How are the first lines the same? When do they change? Can you make an outline of the structure of the poem?

➤ Writing

Time Sequence AM

Use the following structure to plan a selection of your own. Write about a time when you needed help and someone helped you or no one helped you.

Time Sequence Story Map

First . . .

Then . . .

Then . . .

Then . . .

Finally . . .

➤ *Exploring Your Own Experience*

Describe an evening at home.

- Who is there?
- What are you doing?
- What does the room look like?
- How do you feel?

How might this evening change if your country were at war?

➤ *Background*

The following excerpt is from the diary of a 12-year-old girl who, with her family, lived through two years in war-torn Sarajevo, in the former Yugoslavia of Eastern Europe. Like Anne Frank, who called her diary "Kitty," Zlata gave her diary a name, "Mimmy."

Boundaries within the former Yugoslavia as they existed in 1996

Children play volleyball in Sarajevo during a 100-day ceasefire in the spring of 1994.

Zlata's Diary: A Child's Life in Sarajevo

(an excerpt) by Zlata Filipović

Monday, December 28, 1992

Dear Mimmy,

I've been walking my feet off these past few days.

I'm at home today. I had my first piano lesson. My teacher and I kissed and hugged, we hadn't seen each other since March. Then we moved on to Czerny, Bach, Mozart and Chopin to the étude, the invention, the sonata and the "piece." It's not going to be easy. But I'm not going to school now and I'll give it my all. It makes me happy. Mimmy, I'm now in my fifth year of music school.

You know, Mimmy, we've had no water or electricity for ages. When I go out and when there's no shooting it's as if the war were over, but this business with the electricity and water, this darkness, this winter, the shortage of wood and food, brings me back to earth and then I realize that the war is still on. Why? Why on earth don't those "kids" come to some agreement? They really are playing games. And it's us they're playing with.

---

give it my all   try as hard as I can

ages   a very long time

shortage   when there is not enough of something

As I sit writing to you, my dear Mimmy, I look over at Mommy and Daddy. They are reading. They lift their eyes from the page and think about something. What are they thinking about? About the book they are reading or are they trying to put together the scattered pieces of this war puzzle? I think it must be the latter. Somehow they look even sadder to me in the light of the oil lamp (we have no more wax candles, so we make our own oil lamps). I look at Daddy. He really has lost a lot of weight. The scales say twenty-five kilos [55 pounds], but looking at him I think it must be more. I think even his glasses are too big for him. Mommy has lost weight too. She's shrunk somehow, the war has given her wrinkles. God, what is this war doing to my parents? They don't look like my old Mommy and Daddy anymore. Will this ever stop? Will our suffering stop so that my parents can be what they used to be—cheerful, smiling, nice-looking?

This stupid war is destroying my childhood, it's destroying my parents' lives. WHY? STOP THE WAR! I NEED PEACE!

I'm going to play a game of cards with them!

Love from your Zlata.

---

latter   the second thing talked about

ABOUT THE AUTHOR

Zlata Filipović's life changed drastically when war broke out in her home city of Sarajevo, the capital of Bosnia. Her family's weekend house was destroyed, and her close friends were killed in a park. Zlata and her parents left Sarajevo before Christmas in 1993 and moved to Paris.

➤ **Zlata Filipović (born 1980)** ◄

AFTER YOU READ

➤ *What Do You Think?*

1. How is Zlata's evening with her family like yours? How is it different?

2. How do you think war has changed Zlata's life and that of her family?

3. How do you think Zlata feels about the changes in her life?

4. How would you describe Zlata?

5. How would you compare Zlata to Anne Frank (pp. 109–115)?

➤ *Try This*

Comparing and Contrasting with a Chart AM

Use a three-column chart to compare and contrast Zlata and Anne Frank. You might compare/contrast some of these things:

- where they lived
- when they lived
- their families
- how they spent their time at home
- the war they were experiencing

Comparing and Contrasting: Zlata Filipović and Anne Frank		
Aspects of Their Lives	Anne Frank	Zlata Filipović
Where they lived		
When they lived		
Their families		
How they spent their time at home		
The wars they were experiencing		

➤ Learning About Language and Literature

A Paragraph

A paragraph is a unit of thought. Usually a paragraph has a topic sentence that summarizes the paragraph. Usually this is the first or last sentence. Then the paragraph has several sentences about the topic. Always *indent,* or move in about 5 spaces, at the beginning of a paragraph to show the reader where it begins.

1. Look at some paragraphs in *Zlata's Diary* or other selections in this book.
2. How many sentences do the paragraphs have?
3. Can you find topic sentences?
4. Can you find supporting sentences about the topic sentences?

➤ Writing

Comparing and Contrasting AM

Write one or two paragraphs comparing and contrasting two characters from this book or from movies or TV shows. Use a Venn diagram to help you with ideas.

Suggestions:

1. Write a sentence about the two characters you will compare.
2. Write one or two sentences about the first character.
3. Write one or two sentences about the second character.
4. Write a sentence about how they are different.
5. Write a sentence about how they are the same.
6. Write a sentence that summarizes the paragraph.

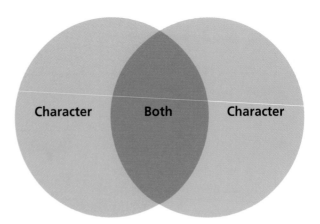

➤ Exploring Your Own Experience

Inside-Outside Circles

Rights are things that all people should be free to do. Going to the church you want is a right. Speaking freely is a right. Voting is a right.

1. What are other rights or freedoms all people should have? Think of at least one.

2. Get into two circles. One circle is inside the other.

3. Inside people ask, "What is one right all people should have?"

4. Outside people answer.

5. Then inside people ask and outside people answer.

6. Inside people move one person clockwise, and everyone asks and answers questions again.

➤ Background

In 1948 people from all over the world came together at the United Nations to make a list of the rights that every human being has, and that everyone should respect. This is the Universal Declaration of Human Rights.

Eleanor Roosevelt holds a copy of the first Universal Declaration of Human Rights.

A meeting of the General Assembly, United Nations

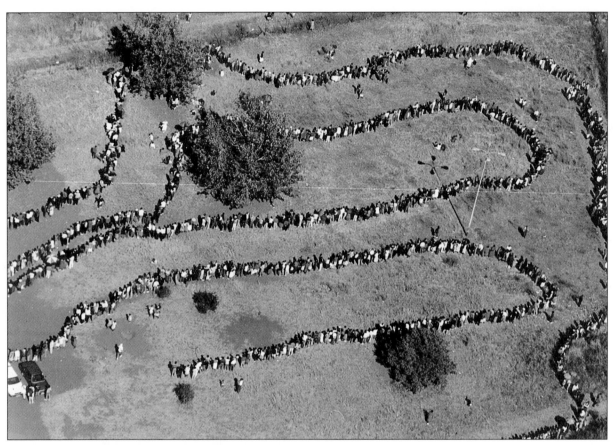

Voters line up for the first multiracial elections in South Africa in April 1994.

The Universal Declaration of Human Rights

Introduction

All people are born free.
   All people are born equal and so
     have equal rights.
   People can think for themselves
   And understand what's going on
     around them.
   Everyone should act as
     Brothers and Sisters.

It doesn't matter what race you are.
It doesn't matter whether
     You're a man or a woman.

It doesn't matter what language you
     speak,
   what your religion is,
What your political opinions are,
   What country you come from or
     who your family is.
It doesn't matter whether you're rich or
     poor.
It doesn't matter what part of the World
     you come from;
   whether your country
     is a kingdom or a republic.

These rights and freedoms are meant to
     be enjoyed by everyone.

---

universal   about everyone
declaration   important statement or
announcement

political opinions   what you think about how
government should work
kingdom   country ruled by a king or a queen
republic   country where people elect rulers

1.

Everyone has the right to live,
The right to be free and the right to
Personal safety.
    No one
    Can be someone
    Else's
    Slave.

Taking an oath of citizenship at the U.S. Immigration and Naturalization Service

2.

No one
Is to be hurt
    Or to be
Punished in cruel
        or
    Humiliating ways.
The law must be the same for
        everyone.
The law must protect everyone.
People have the right to be
        protected by the courts,
        So that their rights are respected.

3.

People cannot be arrested,
        or sent away from their
        country
Unless it's for a very serious reason.
Everyone has the right
        to a fair trial.
No one has the right to interfere in
        other people's private lives,
In their families, in their homes, or
        in their correspondence.
People have the right of free
        movement

---

personal safety   freedom from fear that someone or something will harm you
punished   having something bad happen to you because you did something wrong
cruel   mean, very hurtful
humiliating   in a way that makes someone feel ashamed
protect   keep someone free from harm, take care of someone

respected   paid attention to
arrested   stopped and held by the police
trial   a hearing to find out if someone is guilty of a crime or not
interfere   get in the way
correspondence   letters, mail

A bride and groom in traditional Japanese marriage attire

A minister practicing freedom of speech at The Speakers' Corner, Hyde Park, London

within their country.
People have the right to leave any
country,
Even their own, and then return.

4.

No person or people shall have
Their nationality taken away
from them.
This means everyone has the right
to belong
to a nation.
And they also have the right to
change
Their nationality, if they want to.

All men and women have the right

to get married and start a
family
Once they've reached a certain
age.
It doesn't matter what race,
nationality or religion they are.
A man and a woman can only get
married
If they both want to.

5.

Everyone has the right
to own property.
Anything that belongs to a person
Can't be taken away
From him or her
Unless there's a fair reason.

Everyone has the right to think the
way they like.

nationality belonging to a nation or country

property land, houses, and other things you own

The Universal Declaration of Human Rights **189**

Moslems practicing their freedom of religion at a mosque in Turkey

Association if he or she doesn't
    want to.
A government's
    Authority comes from the will
    of the people.
People must show what they want
    their government to do by
    voting.
Everyone has the right to vote.

7.

Everyone has the right to work.
And people have the right to
    choose
    The kind of job they want to do.
Everyone has the right to
    Good working conditions.
Everyone has the right to equal pay
    For equal work.
People should earn enough to keep
Themselves and their families
    healthy,
    To give them enough food to eat
And enough clothes to wear,
Somewhere to live, and medical
Attention when they're ill.

People have the right to hold
    opinions and tell other
    people what their opinions
    are.
And they have the right to practice
    their religion in
    private or in public.

6.

All people have the right to meet
Together and to form associations.
But no one can be forced to join an

---

opinions   what you think about something
associations   groups of people who want to
do something together

authority   the right to rule over someone
working conditions   what it is like where you
work

8.

Everyone has the right to rest.
They should have a limited number
    of working hours
    And they should still be paid
    While they're on
        Holiday.
All children have the same rights,
Whether their parents are married
    or not.

9.

Everyone has the right
    To go to school
And school must be free.
Everyone should have
    the right to be
    taught a trade.

Education should
Emphasize
    Understanding,
Comprehension,
    Tolerance
And friendship.

10.

People have duties
    Towards the place
    Where they live
And towards other people who
    Live there with them.
Nothing that is written
    In this document may be used
To justify taking away
    The rights and freedoms
Set out in this declaration.

---

emphasize   make important
understanding   when people see each other's meanings
comprehension   knowing what something means

tolerance   allowing other people to believe differently from yourself
duties   special work or jobs, responsibilities
document   important written paper

➤ *What Do You Think?*

1. Why do you think this declaration was written?

2. Which right do you think is the most important? Why?

3. Have you ever seen a situation when people didn't have one of these rights? What happened?

➤ *Try This*

Jigsaw

Use a jigsaw to study the Declaration of Human Rights. In a jigsaw, you divide the work and everyone becomes an expert on one part. Then you teach your part to others.

1. Work in home groups of 4.

2. Each home group member goes to a different expert group. (See the diagram below.)

3. Each expert group studies one part of the Declaration of Human Rights and rewrites that part on a chart.

4. Experts go back to their home groups. Each expert teaches the home group about his or her part of the declaration.

I. From home groups

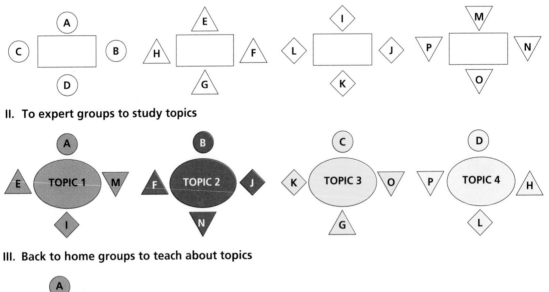

II. To expert groups to study topics

III. Back to home groups to teach about topics

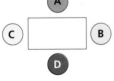

➤ Learning About Language and Literature

Writing Rules and Rights

1. Find a list of rules for your classroom and school.

2. Discuss: How does the writing compare to the writing in the Declaration of Human Rights?

3. Compare your list or the list below with the Declaration of Human Rights.

Class Rules

- *Come to class on time.*
- *Leave gum and food outside.*
- *Bring everything you need to learn.*
- *One person talks at a time.*
- *Use a pass to leave the room.*

➤ Writing

Writing a Declaration of Rights

1. Write a declaration of rights for your class or school.

2. Share your writing with a group of peers, and talk about it.

3. Use the editing checklist to check your writing.

4. Share your final writing with your class.

5. Create a list of five rights that everyone agrees on. Put them on the classroom wall.

Unit Follow-Up

➤ Making Connections

Unit Project Ideas

Here are some possible unit projects. You may also choose to think up a project of your own. Be sure to tell your teacher. Use some of the strategies and concepts you learned in the unit to help you plan and complete your project.

1. Peace Puzzle. Make a peace collage with words and pictures. Cut it up into a jigsaw puzzle. Give the completed puzzle to a younger class for choice-time activity.

2. Peer Mediation. Find a school or class that has peer mediators. Interview a school administrator and a peer mediator to find out about what peer mediators do.

3. Journal. Keep a journal for one month. Tell about your daily events and how you feel about those events.

4. E-Mail. Use a computer message board to ask people from other countries and places about their ideas for peace.

5. Write a Song. Write your own song about peace. You may write new words to a tune you know or make up the tune and the words.

6. Favorite Author Display. Choose your favorite author from *Voices in Literature Bronze.* Use the library and/or CD–ROM encyclopedia to find out more about your author. Make a bulletin board display to share information with the class.

Further Reading AM

Following are some materials related to this unit that you might enjoy.

• ***Chief Joseph: Nez Percé Leader,*** by Marian W. Taylor. New York: Chelsea House, 1993. Chief Joseph bravely resisted the U.S. government and led his people toward a safer home. The Nez Percé traveled over 1,800 miles until they finally had to surrender near Canada.

• ***The Declaration of Human Rights,*** adapted by Ruth Rocha and Octavio Roth. United Nations Publications, 1989. Octavio Roth's prints illustrate the text included in this unit.

• ***A Hand Full of Stars,*** by Rafik Schami, translated by Rika Lesser. New York: Dutton, 1989. An Arab teen in Damascus writes in his journal about himself, his family, and his friends in a war-torn country.

• ***Honey and Salt,*** by Carl Sandburg. New York: Harcourt Brace Jovanovich, 1963. These 77 poems, published when Sandburg was 85 years old, ask important questions on themes of life and love.

- ***I Dream of Peace,*** compiled by UNICEF. New York: HarperCollins, 1994. Writings and drawings by children from the former Yugoslavia vividly reveal the pain and suffering caused by war in their homeland. This book cries for an end to the fighting.

- ***The Nez Percé,*** by Virginia Driving Hawk Sneve. New York: Holiday House, 1994. Historical photographs and paintings help the author tell about the customs and everyday life of the Nez Percé tribe. Europeans gave the Nez Percé their name from their custom of wearing ornaments in their noses.

- ***The Nez Percé,*** by Clifford E. Trafzer. New York: Chelsea House, 1992. This book includes a history of the Nez Percé from the early 1800s, when they first began trading with white settlers, to their present-day life.

- ***Peace Begins with You,*** by Katherine Scholes. New York: Little, Brown, 1989. This book explains how and why peace has a place in all of our lives. It addresses national and international issues of peace, including environmental ones.

- ***A Picture Book of Rosa Parks,*** by David A. Adler. New York: Holiday House, 1993. Robert Casilla's soft-edged color paintings illustrate the story of Rosa Parks's role in the civil rights movement in the U.S. in the 1950s.

- ***Rise Up Singing: The Group-Singing Song Book,*** edited by Peter Blood-Patterson. Bethlehem, PA: Sing-Out, 1988. Words and chords for more than 2,000 songs provide a great source for fun and language learning. Peace songs have their own section, on pages 158–166.

- ***Rose Blanche,*** by Roberto Innocenti. Mankato, MN: Creative Education, 1985. During World War II, a young German girl discovers children held as prisoners in a Nazi concentration camp near her home. She helps keep them alive by secretly bringing them food.

- ***Wind Song,*** by Carl Sandburg. New York: Harcourt Brace and Company, 1960. The poet wrote these 100 poems especially for young readers. Titles include "Buffalo Bill," "Little Girl Be Careful What You Say," and "Frog Songs."

- ***A World in Our Hands: In Honor of the Fiftieth Anniversary of the United Nations.*** Berkeley, CA: Ten Speed Press, 1995. To celebrate the golden anniversary of the United Nations, students aged 7–21 from 115 countries created and edited this history of the organization. The book includes painting, photography, writing, and poetry that explore issues young people care about and paint a vision of the future as they see it.

GLOSSARY

Many of the words in this Glossary have several meanings. We have included only the meanings of the words as they are used in this book.

a

ages a very long time
alighting setting down
arrest stop and take to the police station
arrested stopped and held by the police
association group of people who want to do something together
authority the right to rule over someone

b

beat hit hard, like you hit a drum
blinds window coverings made of many metal pieces that open and close
bolt lock
bounced jumped back, as when you throw a ball against something

c

canyon a place where a river has made a deep cut in the earth
carbon dioxide waste gas from mammals' breathing, necessary gas for plants
Catholic follower of the Catholic religion
chuckling laughing a little
clenched brought together tightly
clothesline a rope for hanging clothes to dry
Communist member of the Communist political group
comprehension knowing what something means
concentration camp prison where people were taken by the Nazis
cook up a storm cook a lot of food
copper reddish-colored metal
correspondence letters, mail

courage bravery
crab sea creature with claws and round shell
creep move very slowly, crawl like a baby
crouch get down low
cruel mean, very hurtful

d

dangling hanging, almost ready to fall off
debt money owed
declaration important statement or announcement
delicious having a very good taste
destroyed ruined, wrecked, made no good
destroying ruining, making no good
didn't take no stuff didn't let people tell her what to do or let them say bad things to her
document important written paper
dough an uncooked mixture of flour, liquid, and other ingredients for baking
duties special work or jobs, responsibilities

e

'em them (dialect)
emphasize make important
encouragement reason to continue
endurance the ability to be strong and last for a long time
ensued happened next
exists is
exorbitant unfairly high

f

faith belief
family tree a picture of all the members of a family and their relationships, in the shape of a tree
fled ran away
flutter move fast up and down or side to side
foggy misty, with clouds low to the ground
fold lay one arm on top of another

forced made to do something without choice

fortune a lot of money—more than enough money to live the rest of your life

g

gather come together

give it my all try as hard as I can

grate use a kitchen tool to shred into small pieces

gutter U-shaped pipe on the edge of a roof to help the rain run off the roof

guayaba (*Spanish*) guava, a tropical fruit

h

hastened hurried

hollow shallow hole or depression in the ground

humiliating in a way that makes someone feel ashamed

i

icebox refrigerator

industry making of goods, manufacturing

insistence taking a stand and not giving it up

interfere get in the way

invention made-up or imaginary idea

j

jammed packed, filled

Jew follower of the Jewish religion

june bug large beetle

k

kingdom country ruled by a king or queen

l

latter the second thing talked about

leapfrog a game in which children crouch down while others jump over them

lifted held up

lilac North American shrub with sweet-smelling lavender (pale purple) or white flowers in the spring

located found

loner a person who likes to be alone

longstanding lasting for a long time

lungs body organs in your chest that help you breathe

m

making ends meet having just enough money to live

mandarin governor of the county

mango a tropical fruit

marbles a game with small colored glass balls

meadows grassland

n

nasty bad, unpleasant

nationality belonging to a nation or country

nizpero (*Spanish*) medlar fruit, a tropical fruit

o

opinion what you think about something

oxygen gas needed for plants and animals to live

p

peek take a little look at

personal having to do with oneself, not for everyone to see or know

personal safety freedom from fear that someone or something will harm you

pitch horseshoes play a game throwing horseshoes so that they land around a metal stake

political opinion what you think about how government should work

private special, not for everyone to see

property land, houses, and other things you own

protect keep someone free from harm, take care of someone

Protestant follower of a Christian religion that is not Catholic

pudding a soft, sweet food made with eggs and milk

punished having something bad happen to you because you did something wrong

r

republic   country where people elect rulers
respected   paid attention to
rhyming   using words ending with the same sound, like *cat* and *rat*
riddle   word puzzle to guess—for example, Q: "Why did the woman throw the butter out the window?" A: "To see the butterfly."
rising   moving upward toward the sky

s

scared   afraid
shack   small, old house
shortage   when there is not enough of something
shrug   move shoulders up
shy   afraid around people, bashful
slave catchers   people who were paid money to catch runaway slaves and return them to their owners
soak   cover with water and leave for a while
solemnly   very seriously
spilled   emptied out, as in "spilled milk"
sprig   very small branch with leaves
survive   stay alive; continue to live
swaying   moving back and forth

t

testify   swear to tell the truth in court and do so
thief   person who steals things

till   until
tolerance   allowing other people to believe differently from yourself
trade unionists   workers who form a group to help improve pay and working conditions
trial   a hearing to find out if someone is guilty of a crime or not

u

understanding   when people see each other's meanings
universal   about everyone
universe   all that there is

w

wave   move back and forth
wealthy   rich
whisper   talk in a very soft voice
wisdom   great knowledge and good judgment
witness   a person who testifies in court about something he or she saw
working conditions   what it is like where you work
working themselves to shadows   working so long and hard that they became very thin

y

yearn   want, long for

ACKNOWLEDGMENTS

Text

Alex Aguilar, "La Siguanava" by Alex Aguilar. Used by permission of the author.

Jorge Argueta, "Miguel en el Norte" by Jorge Argueta. Used by permission of the author.

Byrd Baylor, "The Other Way to Listen" from *The Other Way to Listen* by Byrd Baylor. Copyright © 1978 by Byrd Baylor. Reprinted with the permission of Charles Scribner's Sons.

Dionne Brand, "Rain" and "Hurricane" by Dionne Brand. Copyright © 1979 by Dionne Brand, published by Kids Can Press, Toronto, Canada. Reprinted by permission.

Anne Corkett, "This I Know", "November" and "Unicorn": From *The Salamander's Laughter and Other Poems* by Anne Corkett, copyright © 1985. Reprinted by permission of Natural Heritage/Natural History Inc., Toronto, Canada.

California Department of Education, "Creating Communities of Reformers and Learners from BEOUTREACH, Spring 1994, Volume 5, Number 1. Reprinted by permission.

Fitzhugh Dodson, "Trees Are for Climbing: From *I Wish I Had a Computer That Makes Waffles* by Dr. Fitzhugh Dodson, copyright © 1978 by Oak Tree Publications, San Diego, CA. Reprinted by permission.

Sharon Fear, Mary K. Hawley, Luz Nuncio Schick, "Navajo Code Talkers" from *Foundations* by Sharon Fear, Mary K. Hawley, Luz Nuncio Schick. Copyright © 1991 by Scott, Foresman and Company. "The Surrender Speech of Chief Joseph" from *Foundations for Adult Reading* 2 by Sharon Fear, Mary K. Hawley and Luz Nuncio Schick. Copyright © 1991 by Scott, Foresman and Company. Reprinted by permission.

Carmen Lomas Garza, "Beds Are for Dreaming" from *Family Pictures* by Carmen Lomas Garza. Copyright © 1990 by Carmen Lomas Garza. Reprinted by permission of Children's Book Press.

Toni de Gerez, "Ear of Corn" from 2-RABBIT, 7-WIND; *Poems from Ancient Mexico Retold from Nahautl Texts* by Toni de Gerez. Copyright © 1971 by Toni de Gerez. Reprinted by permission of the author.

Eloise Greenfield, "Harriet Tubman" from HONEY, I LOVE and Other Love Poems by Eloise Greenfield. Copyright © 1978 by Eloise Greenfield. Reprinted by permission of HarperCollins Publishers.

James Houston, From *Songs of the Dream People* (Titled: "A Central Eskimo Chant"), selected and edited by James Houston. Copyright © 1972 by James Houston. Used by permission.

Mattie Lou O'Kelly, "Family Gathering" from *The Hills of Georgia,* An Autobiography in Paintings by Mattie Lou O'Kelly. Copyright © 1983 by Mattie Lou O'Kelly. Reprinted by permission of Little, Brown and Company.

Ruth Rocha and Otavio Roth, "The Universal Declaration of Human Rights" by Ruth Rocha and Otavio Roth. Copyright © 1989 United Nations. Used by permission.

Alvin Schwartz, "When I First Came to this Land" from *And the Green Grass Grew All Around* by Alvin Schwartz. Copyright © 1992 by Alvin Schwartz. Reprinted by permission of HarperCollins Publishers.

U.S. Express, "Science News" from U.S. News, Scholastic Inc. Copyright © 1990 by Scholastic Inc. Reprinted by permission.

Mai Vo Dinh, "The Fly" from *The Toad Is the Emperor's Uncle*: Animal Folktales from Viet-Nam, Doubleday 1970.

Bernard Waber, "The Diary" from Nobody Is Perfick by Bernard Waber. Copyright © 1971 by Bernard Waber. Reprinted by permission of Houghton Mifflin Company.

William Carlos Williams, "This Is Just to Say" from *William Carlos Williams, Selected Poems* edited with an introduction by Charles Tomlinson. Reprinted by permission of New Directions, Inc.

Nancy Wood, "Three Sisters" from *Spirit Walker* by Nancy Wood. Copyright © 1993 by Nancy Wood. Reprinted by permission of Delacorte Press, a division of Bantam Doubleday Dell Publishing Group, Inc.

Richard Wright, "Coming from the Woods" from *Richard Wright Reader* edited by Ellen Wright and Michel Fabre. Copyright © 1978 by Ellen Wright and Michel Fabre. Reprinted by permission of HarperCollins Publishers.

Fine Art/Photos

Cover *Gate of Toledo* by Michio Takayama, ca. 1972–78, Oil on linen, 36 x 30 inches. Courtesy the Jan and Paul Johnson Collection. Artist estate represented by Michael McCormick Gallery, Taos, NM. **2** Erich Lessing/Art Resource, NY., Copyright ARS, NY; **4** Ellis Herwig/The Picture Cube; **5** Bettmann Newsphotos; **6** Frank Siteman/Tony Stone Images; **10** Ricardo Matta/D. Donne Bryant Stock Photography; **12** Canadian Museum of Civilization, Hull, Quebec, Canada by permission of Dorset Fine Arts, West Baffin Eskimo Co-operative Ltd., Toronto, Canada; **18** Art Resource, NY and by permission of Cordon Art; **24** Erich Lessing/Art Resource, NY; **30** University Art Museum, The University of California at Berkeley by permission of The Bearden Foundation, NY; **37** The National Gallery of Art, Washington D.C., photo by John Neubauer; **40–41** Christophe Burki/Tony Stone Images; **43** Marc Muench/Tony Stone Images; **44** Helen Hardin, 1976. Copyright Cradoc Batgshaw 1995. All rights reserved; **46** Courtesy of Nancy Wood, photo by Mary Hayes; **50** Art Resource NY; **53** Courtesy of the National Film Board of Canada; **57** Giraudon/Art Resource; **58** Courtesy of the artist; **60** *top and bottom*, Courtesy of the artist; **61**, *top*, The Bettmann Archive; **61** *middle and bottom*, Werner Forman/Art Resource; **66** David Ryan/D. Donne Bryant Stock Photography; **68** Helen Hardin, 1974. Copyright Cradoc Batgshaw 1995, all rights reserved; **73** *top,* Werner Forman/Art Resource; *Bottom,* Courtesy of Macmillan Publishing Co.; **78** David Barnes/Tony Stone Images; **84–85** Courtesy of The Witte Museum, photo by Jim Zintgraff; **88** Courtesy of the Addison Gallery of American Art, Phillips Andover Academy, Andover, MA; **90** The Bettmann Archive; **93** Tracey Wheeler; **98** Courtesy of Houghton Mifflin Company, Boston, MA; **102** The Bettmann Archive; **104** *left,* The Bettmann Archive; *right,* Jeff Kida for AP/Wide World Photos; **108** AP/Wide World Photos; **110, 111, 112, 114** Museum of Modern Art Film Stills Library; **115** The Bettmann Archive; **122–123** Courtesy of the artist; **125** *right,* Mark Lewis/Tony Stone Images; **126** Museum of Modern Art of Latin America, Organization of American States, Washington D.C.; **132** Reprinted by permission of Little, Brown and Company, Publishers, Boston, MA; **136, 138** Reprinted by permission of The Children's Book Press, San Francisco, CA; **140** Frank Orel/Tony Stone Images; **141** *top,* Courtesy of the Peabody Essex Museum, Salem MA; *bottom,* The Bettmann Archive; **142** Courtesy of Hampton University Museum; **158–159** Art Resource, NY; **161** Stephen Frisch/Stock Boston; **162** *top,* Stuart McClycmont/Tony Stone Images; *bottom,* Scala/Art Resource; **164** The Bettmann Archive; **168** The Bettmann Archive; **174** Courtesy of the artist; **176** Courtesy of The World Council of Churches; **180** Rikard Larma for AP/World Wide Photography; **185** *top,* Sygma News Photos; *bottom,* Courtesy of The United Nations, N.Y.; **186** Gordon Hodge/Sygma News Photos; **188** Ted Soqui/Sygma; **189** *left,* Dennis Stock/Magnum; *right,* J. Pavlovsky/Sygma; **190** Kevin Galvin

Illustrations

Celeste De Coudres: 71

Ruth Flanigan: 9, 14, 48 (right), 131, 166

Peter Reynolds: 21, 22, 23, 28, 34, 35, 38, 49, 54, 55, 82, 87, 93, 116, 147, 177

Colette Slade: 48 (left), 55, 94, 97, 99, 129, 148, 150, 151, 152, 153